let's be REAL

let's be
REAL

Cultivating Authenticity
in a Journey from
Loss to LIFE

Emily Katherine Dalton

NASHVILLE

NEW YORK • LONDON • MELBOURNE • VANCOUVER

let's be REAL
Cultivating Authenticity in a Journey from Loss to LIFE

© 2020 Emily Katherine Dalton

All rights reserved. No portion of this book may be reproduced, stored in a retrieval system, or transmitted in any form or by any means—electronic, mechanical, photocopy, recording, scanning, or other—except for brief quotations in critical reviews or articles, without the prior written permission of the publisher.

Published in New York, New York, by Morgan James Publishing. Morgan James is a trademark of Morgan James, LLC. www.MorganJamesPublishing.com

ISBN 978-1-64279-520-2 paperback
ISBN 978-1-64279-521-9 eBook
Library of Congress Control Number: 2019936245

Cover Design by:
Rachel Lopez
www.r2cdesign.com

Interior Design by:
Bonnie Bushman
The Whole Caboodle Graphic Design

In an effort to support local communities, raise awareness and funds, Morgan James Publishing donates a percentage of all book sales for the life of each book to Habitat for Humanity Peninsula and Greater Williamsburg.

Get involved today! Visit
www.MorganJamesBuilds.com

In loving memory of the best daddy a
"little princess girl" could ever ask for.
I will love you always. Can't wait
to dance with you again.

William Daryl Dalton
1961-2016

Contents

Foreword

*By Dr. Donald J. Wilton, Pastor of
First Baptist Church of
Spartanburg, South Carolina*

The journey is as important as the destination! How many times have we heard this powerful and accurate statement? So true and so important to take hold of. I have said, preached, and dissected this statement in every way possible. Then, there are those that really know this. I present to you Emily Katherine Dalton. Now here is a person I really love and admire. Perhaps a few words will tell you why she means so much to her family, her friends, and all who know her.

I have had the joy of being around Emily Katherine since she was quite a little person. One of the very blessed of blessed girls in this world, Emily Katherine grew up in a most loving family of the highest order. Her mom and dad were just the absolute best parents who doted on Emily Katherine and her brothers, Michael and Andrew. As families go, the Daltons epitomized love, fun, laughter, and just about every experience squashed into their daily habitation. Most certainly Dad married "way over his head" and we all readily agreed because Emily Katherine's Mom is quite the most lovely lady inside and out and in every way. But her dad was a very special man. Devoted, loving, fun, disciplined, hard-working and giving in service to the point at which, those of us who watched him, actually begged him to slow down a little. And then the "cherry on the top" was undoubtedly their commitment to the Lord Jesus Christ. Theirs was an undeniably Christian home in every way. Full of bumps and bruises, no doubt as we all are, but seriously submissive to the Lordship of Christ and to His commission to "go" and serve others in the name of the Lord. Emily Katherine grew up in a faithful family – a family in which the spoken word was matched by the doing word at every level.

And Emily Katherine was Daddy's little girl. Any thought of living out this life without her anchor was, well, not even a thought. Emily Katherine was growing, developing, maturing, and making the most of every opportunity that came her direction. She was actively engaged in her church student ministry and rapidly became a leader in every way. The respect with which her peers held her was remarkable. Her elders just knew this girl was becoming one of God's great leaders for the future. Today it is just plain obvious.

But then it all came crashing down. Her world was turned upside down. Her heart was ripped out and felt like it was being shredded into a million broken pieces. It was so sudden and so unexpected.

God sent His angels down to Spartanburg, South Carolina, on mission. Together they picked Daryl up and gently gave him a royal escort to the feast table of the King of kings and the Lord of lords. Just like that and dad was gone.

None of us can ever imagine pain like this. Not all the assurance of eternal life in Jesus could fill the shrieking pain of this interruption. To be sure Emily Katherine knew exactly where her dad had gone. She knew she had not lost him because Christ had him. But the pain. Excruciating! Deep! Agonizing! And the questions? Where does one begin? Why God, why?

So many are well acquainted with grief. Kathy lives with this grief every day. So do Andrew and Michael. But, perhaps, none like Daddy's little girl.

Thanks for writing this Emily Katherine. We need to hear from you. God has spoken through you to our grieving world. Your words, penned from a hurting heart to the Healer's heart, provides so much comfort for so many.

Introduction

"FAITH CAN LIFT YOU ABOVE YOUR FEARS" proclaimed the church sign I passed in Rome, Georgia. I was driving home just one month after my dad's sudden death. I'd spent the last weeks helping my mom clean her house and fill out life insurance paperwork, and my first post-college job began the next day.

Everything about this church sign stirred all my anger to the surface. Rather than feeling lifted above my fears, they encompassed me in more ways than ever before. The reality of my fears seemed to take greater form than any other realities in front of me. *Who would even go to that church?* I wondered. Should I be in charge of scripting a church sign in my current state, it would most likely read, "Life is just really hard sometimes and there aren't always answers." Because that's what's real.

Church signs, though, are not privileged to honesty. Instead, they often carry the weight of hopefulness and cheer. And I get that. Though the last month has carried doubt of my faith, hurt feelings by fellow church members, and brokenness like I had never felt before, I kept feeling the same weight of forced hopefulness. I kept trying to pull out some cliché, even to make my own life feel more palatable.

But if I let my honesty take full form, nothing feels more hurtful or exhausting than those clichés or the people who have tried to stamp truth on the rawest brokenness I have ever experienced. I have come to learn I am not alone in this. Through honest and real conversations with friends and loved ones, I keep hearing of hurt we have each experienced by the people who start sentences with "At least…" or quote a Bible verse at the worst time.

What my friends and I have come to share with one another is just how deeply we long to be real. To uncover the brokenness, loneliness, hurt, forgotteness, and mess that have felt like an elephant we walk into every conversation, then quietly walk it out when the conversation ends, hoping it went unnoticed. But uncovering what is real with safe people leads to love. And love to hope, even in the darkest places.

As much as I crave love and hope, *real* love and hope are scary and vulnerable. And as I dialogue with friends about this, they agree. I think we hold back from being real, from uncovering our brokenness because it's scary and hard. And on the receiving end of these broken and hard burdens, I think we often offer a cliché or stamp truth because sitting in pain, sometimes hopelessly, feels impossible. As believers who are called to engender hope and joy, holding one another's darkness, rather than trying to shine light on it, can sometimes feel wrong. Other times, I think we hold back from sharing our brokenness and hurt because we feel we shouldn't.

I have had days surrounded by people who love me, bubbling over with pain, but hearing the words in my head I often sing with the four-year-olds I babysit, "Conceal, don't feel. Don't let it show."[1] These lies nudging us to keep hiding have different sources. I have come to name some of mine as my gender identity, self-preservation, and perfectionism. But I have also come to see as a culture we are much better at liking each other's Instagram posts than entering into each other's lives. But the friends who do, the ones who look at you with love when you are overwhelmed with hurt and gently whisper, "I'm sorry," those are the ones who have given me hope to somehow, someday again engender hope and joy.

The same pressure that has prodded me to cover my elephants with my friends or respond to their hurt with the same shallowness, found its way into my relationship with God. As I named my sources of shame and hiding, I saw how

---

1   Menzel, Idina. (2012). Wonderland Music Company. *Let it Go*.

they had become masks I wear to protect myself from the One who knows me best. I began to see evidence of how we all do this as we relate to God.

In my college ministry, we had a newsletter that featured each of the seniors throughout the spring semester. Each senior shared a favorite memory, words of wisdom to their freshman self, and a way to pray for them. Each person's voice was their own as they described something silly they had done or a simple thing they wish they had known, but they seemed to transform into a totally new person when sharing ways to pray for them. Their word choice took on such formality, using words like "guidance, discernment, direction, encounter, behold, challenge," after offering their freshman selves a word of wisdom from a Taylor Swift quote.

And I think I noticed this each and every week on this newsletter posted in my college bathroom because it resonated deeply within me as the exact thing I had grown to do with God. To cover my shame, my hurt, my broken. To muster up the strength to be what I thought He wanted me to be—whole, holy, hardworking, persevering. Yet, I have come to learn those expectations are ones *I* created, not Him. What my Heavenly Father longs for is my authenticity— the real, innermost parts of my heart. To sit in His presence, uncovering all that He already knows, and trusting His grace, love, and mercy will always be enough.

I have found it's that intimacy, that exchange of my insufficiency for His overwhelming sweetness, that causes the most real transformation. Not necessarily saving lives in an unheard-of village, preaching on the most difficult chapter in the Bible, or leading your whole community to Jesus—while those can be beautiful catalysts. For me, the most real transformation stems from the most real encounters.

What you will discover on these pages is that very idea—*intimate transformation*. Transformation that needed to begin in my innermost places, then eventually worked its way to rediscovering friendship and community. But most beautifully amidst it all, rediscovering a God who sees me, knows me, and in my rawest of forms, is exactly who He says He is.

THE REAL ME

Real Me

I led a small group of girls my junior and senior year of college. Each Monday night, the small group leaders met together with a couple who discipled us. One crisp evening as fall showed off its last colors before fading to winter, we decided to meet outside, lying on blankets and praying for those we discipled under a beautiful starry sky in the mountains of Northwest Georgia.

It was a beautiful plan—with one problem. At this time of year, the sun would set around 6:30 pm, an hour and a half before our 8:00 pm gathering. Not only was it dark, but the area we were meeting in was surrounded by many dips and valleys in the ground, making it likely to lose our footing in the darkness. Ever the thoughtful protector, our discipler Chris went to our gathering spot during daylight and placed electric lanterns in every dip and valley of the walk from where we would park to where we would meet.

Grief and trauma have felt like a similar process for me. They have placed lanterns in the dips and valleys where I lose the footing of my faith. Before facing grief, the enemy was faithful to take on the same role, whispering lies that slowly illuminated every dip and every valley until it felt like nowhere was safe to step.

I felt the Lord nudging me to begin this book a year before my dad suddenly passed away from a heart attack and my entire world began to crumble. It's so hard to imagine having written this before that season, before walking back through and falling deep into many of my pits and quickly reaching the end of my rope, hopelessly wondering if I would ever make it out.

If I'm real, I am in a season of hopeless loneliness. Right now I'm reading these words on my computer screen through my all-too-familiar tears. In the past, I usually never had time for the number of people I desired to spend quality time with. But now, in my pits of hopelessness, I feel too broken. This paralyzing fear of letting others see just how broken I am isolates me at a time when I need others the very most.

Annie Down's book *Looking for Lovely*[2] describes her own journey of brokenness and hurt. She writes how a friend shared that her goal should be to be just as real one-foot-deep as she would be thirty feet deep. I froze reading those words, the feeling of such vulnerability impossible to fathom. If I imagined truly saying the words I am wrestling with to others, I honestly only feel safe enough to go about three inches deep.

Of course, there is discernment in how vulnerable to be with which people that requires leaning into wisely. But I cannot keep hiding behind a façade of being okay with the people who are not afraid to enter into my messiness. The fear is my own, of being seen so broken, and worrying if they only knew, they would leave. It feels much more comfortable to be seen in my Instagram posts with filters and clever captions, but no matter how many "likes" I receive, the loneliness still aches and echoes, begging to be seen and cared for, despite how scary it seems.

This battle of being seen in our pits of hopelessness feels even more complicated working in ministry. I have rarely experienced greater tension in my life than serving on a college ministry staff when I was doubting everything I had ever believed about God. We, as believers and as the Church, are the ones who should feel most empowered to live in authenticity, because we know apart from Him, we can

2   Annie F. Downs, *Looking for Lovely: Collecting the Moments That Matter* (Nashville, TN: Lifeway Christian Resources, 2016).

do absolutely nothing; yet, we are the ones who cover our brokenness faster than anyone else. I have been the one on stage Sunday mornings, pushing down my hurts and doubts to appear as though I had it all together, but I've learned someone else who seems to have it all together is the very last thing our fellow believers need. I think it's a key contributor to the brevity of most ministry careers.

We the believers can also be we the broken. We have to be real with ourselves that what we are holding is really hard, that we are not invincible. Our pain does not always feel like a blessing and we absolutely cannot shoulder it alone.

Mosaics, Sewing Machines, and Hammocks

When it comes to crafts or art, I severely lack talent. Many people are quick to diminish their talents or abilities, then excel at those crafts or projects they claimed to be unable to do, and I am absolutely not one of those. I am no Picasso and that is not my kindness or low self-esteem talking.

One time, I was playing a game of Pictionary with friends (already a triggering experience) and needed to draw a dragon. I mustered up all my might and sparse talent to somehow pencil a figure that somewhat resembled a dragon. It is important to know I am terrible at identifying and drawing *standard* animals—cows, ducks, geese, etc.—not to mention mythical ones. My dragon gave my friend Ania such a kick that she still keeps the drawing with her for when she needs a good laugh.

Recently, I again mustered up all of my might and sparse talent, determined to try new things and paint my mom a watercolor canvas for Mother's Day. Of all visual arts (my own personal torture instruments), watercolors seemed to offer the most grace. I painted a solid background on my canvas, reminding myself to breathe. Then came time to create something resembling tulips, because that is what you give your mom for Mother's Day. For once in this artistic process I felt confident. It was like the moment in the movies when someone picks up their secret talent like August Rush picking up his guitar. Finally, my art abilities had found me. As I experienced this gust of empowerment, a friend walked up and with the most genuine tone, asked if the five-year-old next to me painted my watercolor tulips.

This precisely embodies my relationship with art. I remember the first time I discovered my craft handicap when I was in the third grade. Looking back on early elementary school years, I am amazed we all made it through. If I were forced to sit in the same place from 8 am to 3 pm, with only a couple restroom breaks and twenty minutes to eat and talk to my friends, I would form revolts the history books would talk about for generations to come. What challenged me most in elementary school was art class. I suppose all children are created in God's image and have a creative gene, but in 2001 my art teacher at Westover Christian Academy in a small, southern Virginia tobacco town was yet to discover my creativity is best expressed in graphic design.

At the time, I was really interested in butterflies, to the degree that each week during library class (one of the less oppressive parts of elementary school), I checked out the book *What is a Butterfly?* Every singly Friday. When Mrs. McKenzie stood before our art class and instructed us to create a mosaic (after explaining what a mosaic was), I immediately knew my mosaic would be the most beautiful butterfly the world had ever seen. In my eight-year-old eyes, the butterfly I drew looked precisely like the orange one on the cover of my favorite read.

Next, Mrs. McKenzie instructed us to draw a grid on our picture, cut out the pieces, transfer them to a piece of construction paper, and glue the pieces on, mirroring a mosaic (this is a Christian school budget here). While my original butterfly had all of my confidence, this grid-drawing and transferring process had none. I could blame this on my lack of art abilities, but if we are honest, a big part of the problem was my lack of focus because I love to talk to the people around me a little too much.

Week after week, I came back to this sad little butterfly cut up into pieces with absolutely no clue how it was originally ordered. As I sought to salvage the wreckage of each orange piece and glue a few defeated pieces onto construction paper, I wanted to cry. Mrs. McKenzie came over and tried to help me lay the pieces back out where they belonged. It looked terrible. Absolutely terrible.

This butterfly mosaic was in no way presentable. Fine Arts Night was around the corner, and there was no way my terrible butterfly mosaic would be pinned to the felt walls of the foyer for parents to view and gush about how talented their child was. If Mrs. McKenzie pinned my mosaic on the wall, her job would be at risk; it was that terrible. I can still feel my throat closing as I stared at my poor orange butterfly, wanting to both throw up and cry. As I sat red-faced in my little, third-grade-art-class chair, I did all I could not to cry. My art project was terrible. I was terrible. I would never do art again.

In middle school, I decided to pick up sewing. A machine did the work for me; I mean, how hard could it be? My small tobacco town lacked many things, including a craft store, so my family took me to Wal-Mart to get a sewing machine for Christmas, along with a blanket that would be my first project. My poor mom and I sat at the sewing table for hours, trying to figure out this project. I had no clue what I was doing, or even really how to tie a knot. Everything was messed up, so I gave up. I'd barely started the blanket, and it was already in ruins. I boxed it up and put it away and would never sew again. The blanket was imperfect. I was imperfect.

During Christmas break of my freshman year of college, my dad and I walked around an outdoors store. I was attending Berry College in Rome, Georgia, the world's largest college campus made up of beautiful mountains and hiking trails. As we passed a hammock I had been wanting, I commented on its great sale price. My dad bought it and told me if I played my cards right, Santa would bring me the hammock for Christmas. Thinking of his kindness and generosity now brings tears to my eyes, but in the moment when I should have only been thankful and excited, I felt sick to my stomach. That feeling from third grade art class swelled back up inside of me. All I could think of was how I would never use it enough, how I could never be a good enough hammock owner, and would probably be too embarrassed of messing up that I would never use it.

Standing in the checkout line at Mast General Store in Downtown Greenville, South Carolina, I realized a problem I had been living with my entire life—*perfectionism*.

I hated my butterfly in Mrs. McKenzie's art class, not just because of how bad it looked, but because of how terribly it paled in comparison to the mosaics of my classmates. My mosaic was not perfect. It fell greatly short of the image in my head I had dreamt up for my orange butterfly mosaic. Never sewing again was in no way for a lack of trying, rather because I never had my August Rush moment of picking up a skill and immediately executing it perfectly. The standards I had set for myself were so much higher than how I had performed in art class, in sewing, and soon to be as a hammock owner. It was paralyzing.

When what I did failed to meet my standards, I believed *I* did not meet them either. And if others are not complimenting me on my performance, then they will see who I really am. A failure. And I cannot stand it, so I push myself, even at times into the ground, to have it all together—or at least, be perceived in such away.

Yet, perfectionism never drives us to a state of homeostasis, rather a constant state of striving more diligently and exhaustedly. A perfectionist like myself will work and work until we feel somewhat safe, hidden behind the excellence of our performance.

My freshman year of college this fear of failing was right before my face time after time as I saw the boldness of those around me to attempt new things, yet I felt paralyzed by knowing I could never execute them perfectly. Despite my fear, I learned from those same bold friends that when I did try and I did fail, they loved me all the same. Through their boldness, courage, and security in who they were apart from their striving and mine, we were enough together. Behind our walls of performance and shame, they saw me and taught me I never had to be perfect. Ania's drawing of my dragon is not a place of shame for me, but a consistent reminder of the way Ania always looks at me the same on my best days and my worst, as a friend.

Perfectionism limited me not only from trying new things, but from truly knowing myself. A perfect person has no flaws, and to maintain this belief I had to hide from the faults in myself and my life that were shouting to be heard and acknowledged in my heart and mind, yet so hidden from myself and others. The broken parts of my story and my heart were left unacknowledged and dismissed, yet these elements of who we are always find a way of being acknowledged, whether we are ready or not.

Truly getting to know the real me took unraveling my perceived perfectionism. I distinctly remember some of the first times I allowed myself to think what I was actually thinking and feel what I was actually feeling, laying down the expectation to be perfect in my mind. Of course there is a line of guarding our minds, but when I reconnected to my true self, not the self I had tried to create, I found a freedom I never knew existed.

Freedom. Freedom like I never thought possible, but getting there was hard and messy. When I began to choose myself over everyone else's expectations, I let them down. A friend and mentor shared with me in this season that this sorting of who we are and who we will be is similar to rearranging furniture in your home.

If a friend comes over expecting to plop right down on the couch they have always sat on, they will jarringly fall to the ground, frustrated the couch is not where it always was. There is no propelling force for this people-pleasing perfectionist like avoiding letting someone down, but I learned to understand that it is my house and my furniture, and not only do I get to choose when to open the door, I am the one responsible for the furniture when everyone else goes back to their own. I determined that shame would not win any longer, no matter how hard the journey would be.

And while the journey is a treacherous one, it was a worthy one. And your journey will be too, because you are worthy. You are worthy to no longer let shame win, keeping you from yourself and the beautiful things of life beyond your standards of achievement and performance. You are worthy on your worst day. And I am too.

Be Ladylike

When I was in fourth grade, my class took a field trip to Jamestown. Growing up in Virginia provided a variety of unique opportunities to experience key places in United States history close to home. In Jamestown, we sat in a simulation of a traditional schoolhouse for the children of the early colonial era. The boys were permitted to sit however they wanted, but the girls were instructed to hold a penny between our knees to be sure we kept our legs together without crossing them. We all tried our hardest to do this for only one minute, then had to stop because it felt so unnatural.

One of the interesting facets of adulthood for me has been recalling and considering phrases I heard repeatedly in my developmental years. I tend to still hear these phrases in my head such as, "Rub some dirt in it." And, "A friend in need is a friend in deed." A key one that often comes to mind for me, especially in my shame spiral is, "That's not very ladylike!" I mean, it's not my fault. I grew up with two older brothers and wanted to be exactly like them to the point that when people asked me what I wanted to be when I was little, I responded, "Six feet tall." My mom is a nurse who left for work early in the mornings, so my sweet dad dressed me, styled my hair, and cooked dinner for my family. Spending so much time with two brothers and my dad taught me a great deal about manhood and very little about this obscure concept of being ladylike, other than knowing I was surely doing it wrong.

Recently, my family went on vacation and my brother Michael created a workout for my friend Emily, who was traveling with us, and me. (It is important to note that in our family Michael received all of the fitness genes.) While Michael is a seasoned and talented athlete, Emily and I were solely seeking a good workout. We did exactly as Michael coached us, though he had heavier weights and more repetitions of all the exercises we did. While Michael is in much better shape than Emily and I, by the end of our workout he was leaning over, feeling sick to his stomach, and Emily and I smiled through the whole workout.

No, I was in no way smiling on the inside. Rather, I think for Emily and me we were following the social codes our gender had taught us. These codes that can be so oppressive, limiting, and unnecessary. We, as girls, have learned to smile through pain, often shaming ourselves for facing it at all.

I grew up in a church that rarely emphasized women in Scripture, so I just followed the codes of gender I observed from the women in my church. Codes sometimes whispered, such as making sure to use your manners and cross your legs. But some codes shouted, like when all the girls were told not to answer all the questions in Sunday school because they boys' growth in their faith was more important. I wish I was exaggerating. In my most formative years, these codes of gender shaped and formed my faith, and in doing so shaped me. Not only did I always feel I was falling short of being ladylike, it felt like a cage I wanted to run with all of my might to escape from.

Then, I learned this version of being "ladylike" was not true biblical femininity at all. The Columbine school shooting in Littleton, Colorado, took place on my fifth birthday. I remember coming home from school and my family crowding around the television, watching the terrible news of what had happened. Growing up in the faith community, two key stories surfaced from this shooting about two girls who stood up for their faith, even though it cost them their lives. Two girls. Cassie and Rachel. By the faithfulness of Jesus, their memoirs were finished and released around the time my reading level could understand them. As a fourth grader, I would sit in my room and pour over *She Said Yes* and *Rachel's Tears*, amazed by these two high school girls' courage and bravery, and so refreshed from reading of heroines of the faith.

While Cassie and Rachel inspired me, the beliefs that the Christian faith was first for men was deeply seeded in my spirit until years later, when I found another heroine sitting on the roof of my church's youth building. My family moved to South Carolina when I was in sixth grade and became a part of an incredible church that has been such a blessing to us. My youth leader at the time, who I now call a best friend, hosted us on the roof of the youth building with a tent and a cooler full of Sprite, and had us open our Bibles to John 4.

I had been in the Church since before my birth and always attended a Christian school. Most stories in Scripture were familiar to me, and I was expected to just be reminded of a story I knew, rather than introduced to one. Instead, my whole world changed. As I sat in the warmth of a South Carolina summer night and the sun set over our youth building in downtown Spartanburg, Jillian unpacked the longest dialogue between Jesus and another person recorded in Scripture—and that other person was a woman. The Woman at the Well. Yes, I knew her story, but for the first time, her true humanity took form to me. This woman, shamed for her culture, her past, and her gender, did not hold back one bit from being exactly who she was with the Messiah. When He inquired of her to give Him a drink of water, she sharply responded, "You don't even have a bucket."[3] (I'm paraphrasing.)

As I saw her freedom to relate to herself and literally the Savior of the world despite her past and her gender, I began to claim some of that very freedom for myself. I stopped blaming myself for running from the cage of femininity I had seen. Because as this woman was so real with Jesus, He never backed away and never shamed her. He just kept pressing in deeper and deeper to know her true self beneath each of the walls she'd worked so hard to build and hide behind.

If I ever have a daughter, I will probably still teach her what it means to be ladylike. She will know her manners, sit with her legs together, and say "Yes, ma'am" and, "No, sir," but over my dead body will she ever be a told her faith or her presence are less important than the boy sitting next to her.

In learning to allow the real me to be seen and known, I had to first decode the many messages I still hear in my head, many rooted in gender. Jesus is faithful to me, in that I have never wrestled with my gender identity or sexuality, while I know so many have walked on this difficult and isolating journey. But I have had to fight to chip away at walls I hid behind, many in the Spirit of "being ladylike." I am still learning to believe that I am more than how I look and the attention I receive. I am still learning to find my voice and to stick up for myself, no matter who I am around. I am still

3   John 4:11

fighting to create a culture of women who can be real with one another, so one of us is not walking to the well in the heat of the day while all the others shame her.

My sisters, you are not a doormat. You have a voice and a backbone that are yours to wield for the glory of the Kingdom of the Most High that includes both genders. You are so much more than an object for a man's pleasure. You have been given a brain to think and dream, to create, to nurture, and to mirror the immaculate glory of the Creator who fashioned you. You are more than your dress size and the composure you keep that everything's fine when you are truly dying on the inside. Nothing about your biological sex keeps you from being human and feeling pain and hurt. Your faith matters. Jesus sits with you. He reveals Himself to you. Don't hide like I did.

And to my brothers, you are more than a machine made to accomplish. You have been given a heart to create, to feel, and to hold the weight of emotions, just as the Savior who created you both acted in courage and wept in brokenness. We ladies, do no need you to keep it together for us. In fact, so many of us are desperate for you to be real with yourself and us about what is truly going on in your hearts. You are more than the muscles you build. You are more than the dollar signs in your bank account. Your presence, your unproductive presence, is of the utmost value. God addresses both your courage and your fear, both your joy and your brokenness. There is great purpose in your fragility.

I have watched the enemy use gender roles for his glory in the Church for far too long. In my grief, the anger that was raging inside of me felt wrong and I had no clue how to express it. The night my dad had his heart attack and lie unconscious in cardiac intensive care, my brother Michael and I walked to the car to get something. He humbly shared, "It's just so hard because I feel like because I'm the oldest brother, I should have it more together or something. I feel like I should be brave, but I'm terrified. I'm a mess right now." And I have never been more proud of him than in that moment.

Whether we have been fashioned and formed as male or female, we all have emotions and feel anger and pain because we are all human. And the core of that humanity, the defining feature of our flesh and bones, is not the sexuality that culture has told us reigns supreme. Rather, it is the glory of God, our Father, Creator, and Sustainer singing of His goodness, intentionality, and creativity in every fiber of marrow, every cell, and each and every hair on our heads.

That's Really Real, Girl

I sat in a large armchair next to a coffee table in a small room, clutching a throw pillow, holding a tissue box in my counselor's office, spilling feelings and hurts until this moment I had never allowed myself to claim. Unloading the deepest of wounds felt like the scene in *Princess Diaries* where Mia and her mother launched darts toward balloons full of paint. As each balloon was struck, it burst open, splattering paint all over the canvas. Naming these lifelong hurts and wounds felt like launching darts toward each balloon that weighed heavier and heavier, protecting the canvas of my life I fought to keep clean and white. Each naming, each launch of every dart felt wrong, and once the words escaped my mouth, I felt I deserved some kind of punishment for even thinking such a thing, but my dear counselor was never surprised. She looked me in my scared eyes and said tenderly through her tears, "That makes sense." Sometimes she laughed in amazement at my candidness.

A large part of my story is *adultification*, which technically is not a word, but the idea that in my young age, important people in my life perceived me as capable of caring for myself physically and emotionally sooner than I was truly ready. This experience was due to a mixture of circumstances surrounding my childhood, including being a third child and parents facing advances to their careers along with pursuing graduate school during some of my key developmental years. Apart from these circumstances, I did grow up quickly, learning to speak in complete sentences before I was two and helping around the house around four or five, mostly because I wanted to.

Adultification needs to happen at some point, and some children grow up never experiencing any independence, lost as to how to carry themselves when adulthood sets in. But adultification sent me a few messages that I took to the extreme. Messages that told me being a little girl was too much of a burden, having needs would send everyone around me over the edge, and when I did not understand something, I needed to fake it. Trust me, I caused *plenty* of moments of drama, ridiculousness, and selfishness that every member of my family and extended family can attest to. But these messages carved themselves deeply into my heart, forming grooves that were interwoven with my very identity and personality; that is, until everything hit the fan.

The beauty of childhood was lost on me a little too early. The safety of children feeling they could fearlessly ask any question in the world was a safety I became unfamiliar with all too soon. The faith to throw themselves at whatever they felt passionate about at the moment, no matter the outcome, was significantly smaller for me. This freedom and ability to take from everyone, needing love and begging for affection so much more resembled shame for me.

One time, my seven-year-old body woke up restless in the middle of the night. With tears streaming down my face, I frantically shook my mom to wake her up, my face overcome with the fear of how I would pay my taxes one day. Call this childhood anxiety or adultification, but while every other seven-year-old girl was dreaming about which American Girl Doll accessory they would shop for next, I was estimating my future net worth.

As I learned to hide my needs and desire for attention, I learned to compensate by meeting the needs of the world around me. First thing in the morning, I was absolutely a little girl. My sweet dad would wake me up over and over, singing the same song about birds, yet I lie there, unmoved. Finally, he would give up hope of me cooperating, gently pull me out of bed, dress me, and carry my sleeping frame to the table. Still fast asleep, he placed a bowl of cereal in front of me. I promise I am still this bad at mornings, it's just that now there is coffee.

In my elementary school, I was never the prettiest or the smartest girl. As the youngest child with two older brothers and someone who was dressed by my dad every morning, I rarely wore the cutest outfits; rather, I mostly wore hand-me-downs from my neighbors. My teachers never doted on me like they did the other girls when they walked in the classroom with their perfectly styled hair and beautiful outfits, so I learned to win their attention by helping. You could always find me first in line to alphabetize papers, organize bookshelves, or complete whatever task my teacher needed accomplished. I learned to stop asking questions when I could not understand my homework, because I so desperately craved their affection.

After school, my brother Andrew and I argued endlessly about what to watch on television. When my dad came home from work, I helped cook dinner. My dad told me how to help him and walked me through each step as he did most of the work then handed me the bowl and spoon to stir. Despite my small contributions, I was convinced I had made every dish.

Helping and striving for attention became the very fabric of my DNA, my motivation in all that I sought, worked for, and hid from. Looking back now, I can see the enemy's purpose and intentions at the heart of it all. While everything I experienced was simply normal at the time, I can now see moments when he swooped in to groove those messages on my heart a little deeper. And I lost myself in this.

If I'm being real, I can count about fifteen years when I was not completely sure what I even liked to do or what my personality was like. I lost touch with myself to find a girl everyone else would give affection to, a girl who made room for everyone else's needs in her heart, and in turn, lost my very own.

The enemy whispered to me over and over to stop fighting. Stop standing up for myself. Just be easy to get along with. Just be what everyone needs.

But my Father never stopped fighting for me. Not the *me* I had worked so tirelessly to create, but the forgotten little girl deep inside of me. As I read the words on the pages of the book of John about a woman at a well who laid all of her sass on the table with Jesus, my Father gently called that little girl out of hiding. This woman of a race that no one approved of, stood her ground and asked her questions and Jesus did not back down for a second. She was not too much for Him to handle. She never lost His favor or approval. Jesus invited me to take off my layers and walls of perfectionism, striving, and people pleasing and to just be a little girl asleep and hungry at the breakfast table with Him. He invited me to show up in His presence just as fearlessly as the Woman at the Well.

As I felt the mercy in Jesus' eyes for this woman, the little girl inside of me felt free to be seen and known for the first time in a long time. And as she stepped out in all of her messiness and vulnerability and told me she needed to come out of hiding, I could only affirm just as Jesus did with the woman at a well in the middle of the afternoon, "That's really real, girl."

Boxes

I keep hearing that word in my head over and over. *Boxes*. I often hate the necessary role they play in life. They carry transitions. They are one of the first items to purchase when making a move in life, whether big, such as crossing oceans and countries, or small, such as simply moving down the hall. They are a way of consolidating, simplifying, compressing, and efficiently transitioning.

Boxes mark other transitions, like on Christmas morning. Box after box brings new items that will now be a part of your life and routine. Boxes fill a living room where a baby shower anticipates a new little one. Boxes pile up on a gift table at a wedding reception, celebrating that two are becoming one. Boxes are a part of our lives because transitions are.

And a box is where we end. We experience transition after transition until we reach the final one from life to death. And there is one last box. I hated that room at the funeral home. That room of boxes, or coffins rather. We were walked down a carpeted hallway to a room full of them. Wooden, metal, ornate, and plain. Boxes, like it even matters. I hated the reality of it. I hated that we were choosing one for my dad's body. I hated that we were now handling the logistics of his body. I didn't care what the box looked like that he would be laid in to rest, I just wanted him back, and so many days I still do. Yet there was a decision to be made and there was a box to choose because these hard transitions don't give us a choice. They force us to one. But I couldn't handle the weight of that day and that moment, so I stood at the entrance to the door and held my breath to be able to hold anything together.

And there's a box on the bookshelf next to my bed that my dad built for me my sophomore year of college. I love how this bookshelf represents him and bears his image in my room. The box that rests on the bookshelf holds so many pieces of my dad—a letter he wrote, a few photos of us, a diaper with my name in his handwriting—all I could consolidate in one place to have a small piece of him. My little box of him.

But this box is different.

This isn't a box that marks a transition, that moves things more efficiently to the next step. This is a box I will reopen time and again and treasure and never truly use for a practical purpose that boxes so often serve.

And I've had to make that very transition in many areas of my life.

I have desperately wanted to keep my emotions in a box. And I did for a long time. I mastered always being okay so no one else had to be. Then my world was thrown upside down. I took my experiences and emotions and immediately packed them away, rather than experiencing them. And while my life looked tidy, I wasn't building a life or a home. I was building a warehouse, a warehouse of many items I never knew.

I became so skilled at packing my feelings away, it became a subconscious act. But grief did a wild thing to me. It came in, tore open every box, dumped their contents all over the floor, and asked me to go and sit in the mess. To pick up and hold many of the items one at a time, some I barely recognized, but each a significant part of my life.

I think we all have ways of storing what we're handed, rather than holding it. I think it's part of why the Woman at the Well came to Jacob's well in the heat of the day.

Last week I became so emotional in the church parking lot, I called a friend and cried into his chest for thirty minutes. A year ago, I would have barely let him see me tear up. Today, I wept with the accountant in my office, when my staff collected money to help me pay for the $300 ticket I got driving a company car. And tonight, I fumed when my cat peed all over a bed and it took four cycles of washing to clean.

Living on autopilot feels like a safer way to walk through life emotionally. But I hate living out of boxes, like the ones we call suitcases. When I travel, I put my things in the drawers and closets of my hotel room. I spread my hair wand and toothbrush on the bathroom counter because the last thing I want to feel on vacation is like it's a constant transition. I want to feel at home.

And I'm learning to feel at home in the messiness. I think I will always be unable to go to sleep with dirty dishes in the sink and I make my bed more days than I don't, but I am learning to hold what I'm handed. And sometimes that means little messes. But in the same way we don't shame a toddler for spilling their juice on the carpet when they had to drink out of a big-person cup, I don't think God is shaming me for making some messes when I've had to drink out of some real big-people cups this year.

I'm learning to sometimes say no to things I'm asked to hold, when before I would have always said yes. I had the capacity to take and store what was handed to me, but I never had the capacity to actually hold it, feel it, and embrace it.

I'm learning to be hurt by what's handed to me. I had reached a point of choosing to be chronically unoffended.

I was significantly hurt by people, disrespected, and overlooked, but I chose to store it as a way to help someone down the road. I was told that was wisdom. Rather, that was sowing seeds to later harvest bitterness.

If I'm honest, I've been handed too much to hold already this week and it would be easy to pack it all away. I would love for the anxious dreams to stop, to have a complete appetite, and to not constantly walk around wishing someone would hug me. But what's real is not a life that looks like a warehouse. Sitting, holding, embracing, loving, and grieving our things before we embrace the transitions that call us to put them into boxes is living. It's making a home and making a life that makes that very last box all the more meaningful, significant, and real.

Empathy Crier

All my friends' bio sections on their social media accounts included fun descriptions such as, "loud laugher" or, "practical creator." For the longest time, my bio proclaimed, "empathy crier." This felt like the most fitting first impression to greet someone who may not know me by saying, hi there, I may not know you now, but I am going to care deeply about you. After all, I often found myself sitting with friends and listening to them share their hearts.

And while this felt like a fitting first impression that many others would attest to, I knew deep in my soul being this selfless, caring person was much more of an aspiration than a description of me. This aspiration, this person I longed to be who threw herself into other people's hurts and felt the depths with them, was not exactly a noble inspiration, but a way of hiding. My insecurity could not be stifled to stay quiet, but instead filled my planner with coffee dates, volunteer commitments, weekly expectations, and daily obligations to somehow lose track of myself, who I was so afraid of being. Because she was never enough. I felt terrified to just show up, without being needed. This fear and insecurity loved the people around me tenaciously, while the real me was anxious and stressed, carrying around a back full of knots, and lonelier than I ever knew how to admit. What now sounds like an exhausting prison was the safest identity I knew.

This strategy the enemy employed against me is a common one, shooting straight for the core of who we are. How effective he is to aim his arrows directly at our identity. As I attempted to form some new version of myself that could show up no matter how unimportant, my counselor read me a beautiful quote. As each word reached my ears, I felt more and more revealed, and honestly a little afraid someone had read my journal. This quote explained when we do not allow people to see the real us, we send our representatives forward.

I had to remind myself to breathe, and I still tighten up when I hear it.

At this point, I was not even sure who I was for the sake of my representatives. I had groomed and shaped them to be what everyone else needed, while forgetting who *I* was. Forgetting I even existed, really. All I cared about was those representatives and how they appeared. They were the only Emily Katherine the world knew, and the only Emily Katherine I had known as well.

The Woman at the Well seems to employ a similar strategy in order to survive the shame of showing up at the well the day she ran into Jesus. Her true self experienced so much hurt, disrespect, and disregard. I imagine working up the nerve to walk to get the water she needed to survive each day left her questioning if living without water or facing the shame of her community would be harder. So she sent her representative forward, a representative who upon facing Jesus responded in a way that illuminated her walls. She presumed Jesus would treat her just as all the other men in her community had. "You have no bucket." She threw at Him when He asked to draw water.

As He spoke and revealed His knowledge of the Kingdom of God she said, "Sir, aren't you a prophet?" And when He asked her to go and call her husband, the words shot through her representative to her true self. Again, her walls shot up, "Sir, I have no husband." Because she had five previous husbands and was living with a man whom she was not married to.

A good way to describe my representatives is as my guardians. My guardians protected me to the degree I believed they were all I was. The enemy shot a bull's eye, attacking me at my core to twist the very gifting God placed in me to love those around me selflessly.

My counselor encouraged me to befriend my true self, to stop pushing down what she needed and felt, and meet her with the same grace and compassion I would anyone else. To no longer tell her she was not enough and to offer sympathy for all she had walked through.

There's a god in the movie *Moana*, one with the power to give life based on her little green, glowing heart. But Maui, a demigod, wants her power, so he comes and steals her heart. Without this heart, rather than giving life, she gives darkness. It spreads and infests every island, taking over its resources and beauty. But when Moana and Maui embark on a quest to return the heart, they face great difficulty. Moana looks into the god's eyes and says, "This is not who you are." The green heart is returned, and all is right again.

I can't compare myself to a god who gives life, nor am I condoning any pantheism, but I think the enemy came and took the tenderness of my heart. He told me that was who I was. That if I cared for and served as a safe place for every single person around me well enough, I would finally *be* enough. If I cared enough for everyone around me, no one would see the real me. It became who I was, until I couldn't anymore. And when I couldn't anymore, I was lost.

I have learned to welcome and befriend my true self, but it first required firing my guardians and representatives. I could no longer value everyone's needs to the degree I overlooked valuing myself. I had to let the girl who was willing to be all things to all people go, because my counselor told me if I kept living at this pace, I would die very young. I am scared to say she was right.

I had to learn to let people down for the real me to show up. And when the real me can show up, I cry empathetically with people. I cry at their pains and their celebrations. I jump in and feel what my people are feeling, in a more real way than ever before, because one of my representatives is not mustering up tears for them. My heart breaks with them. To be an authentically tender self, I have to take some appointments off my insecurity's calendar, which removes a few knots from my fear's back.

REAL FRIENDS

Miranda Lambert, David,
and Jonathan

I am unsure if these three people have ever been categorized together. Bible heroes David and Jonathan are often grouped together, but adding Miranda Lambert in there I imagine is a bit like adding anchovies to a peanut butter and jelly sandwich. These three characters' dynamic seems hard to fathom, with stories that seem difficult if not impossible to interweave. Family can be the same way.

To know me well is to know I am Southern, quick to ask you about your heart, a toucher, and a reader. To know me well is to also know my brothers.

Michael is six years older than me, a CrossFit coach, fierce lover of all things American, a presence that doesn't quietly fade into the background, an achiever, a motivator, a creative, and an organizer.

Andrew is two and a half years older than me, but he always argued it was three when we were growing up. He's an English teacher, a conspiracy theorist, a lover of literature, an out-of-the-box, big-brother's-got nothing-on-me, challenger of social norms, and a dog lover.

We are three very different people, united primarily by a love for coffee, La Croix, and *New Girl*.

We don't make sense, yet amidst our eclectic dynamic we form a family. This tight unit is meant to be "born for adversity" and oh, has it been in this past year. And while family can be the safest and most caring places, it can also be the hardest.

I love Miranda Lambert's song, *Mama's Broken Heart*.[4] Lambert sings of a broken heart manifesting in a small, southern town, perfectly explaining the experience. The song describes her heartbreak as it echoes through her home and beyond. Reeling from her broken heart, Miranda's bold chorus recounts her mom's demands to freshen up and

4   Clark, Brandy, McAnally, Shane, and Musgraves, Kasey. (2013). RCA Nashville. *Mama's Broken Heart*.

calm down to save face—every southern girl is nodding in agreement to this experience. But the tagline of the chorus is that this broken heart is Miranda's to hold, not her mom's.

Her mom is minimizing her pain, seeking to mitigate her outbursts that are so very raw. While Miranda is expressing the brokenness of her bleeding heart, her mom spotlights the image she is presenting to all of her onlookers. Many of us we were raised to appear to keep it all together when everything falls apart, but sometimes we *are* what's falling apart, and our mess trickles from behind closed doors.

I resonate with this song deeply, as I do with a few too many country songs, considering my upbringing. In a small town, word does get around quickly, especially amongst those who tend to always be the ones to spread the word. And often whose phone is "ringing off the hook" (for those younger than me, phones used to be attached to a hook, so when they rang a lot they would fall off. In modern day terms, everyone was blowing up my mom's phone.) is Mama, or anyone in your family for that matter.

And I love the stance Miranda takes in this song. She doesn't apologize for her crazy. She simply says, "No, Mom. This is my broken heart to feel." And her feelings are valid.

I don't condone cutting your own bangs or a few of the other crazy things in this song. But there are a lot of times our family asks us to "hide our crazy," whether it is communicated explicitly or through various demands. For some of us, it has been for the very reason stated in the song:

to "start acting like a lady." For others, we had to hide our crazy to "keep a spotless reputation." And for some, we were never allowed to let our crazy surface because we just had to move on and face the next demand life brought.

And while family was originally intended to be a safe place for each of us to grow, and a place for us to be known, loved, nurtured, and cared for on our best days and our worst, for many of us, family feels like the place we have to "save a little face" the most. I think this is why everyone is so desperate to get home to a glass of wine after a family Christmas dinner, coping with the pressure and exhaustion of choosing each and every word so carefully as countless questions are launched your way from the people who supposedly love you most. If I'm real, I hate it.

I hate it because I desperately desire to honestly bear my mistakes with my family, but it's hard. I want to honestly bear the growth I've walked through and the things I've learned about myself, but one of the scariest places to bear such progress is in a room full of the faces looking at me whose eyes have seen and known you every day of my life.

The lack of vulnerability permeates not only within our families, but in how we communicate about our families to the world around us. Somewhere along the way, something taught us to be loyal to this idea that your family is always good, no matter how much of a lie that is, choosing to look like the Brady Bunch over the Kardashians every day, no matter what happens behind closed doors and is discussed over the phone afterward. And if I'm real, processing my own story with my family took years of pushing it down, afraid of all the Kardashians in our home, held to the Brady standard.

And I have learned so much from Jonathan and David in this. Jonathan is Saul's son and Saul is the King of Israel. But the people of Israel are unhappy with Saul, desiring that David would be made King. This is a conflict of interest for Jonathan both because David is his best friend and because Saul is trying to kill David. While Jonathan truly felt the pressure to be loyal to his family, especially as the royal family, when Saul was seeking to kill David, Jonathan remained a great friend to him, warning him of Saul's schemes, and ultimately saving his life.[5]

Sometimes being real with people means letting them into the crazy of your family. Sometimes you need to protect your family, but sometimes we need to stop sending as many Christmas cards with starched collars and smiling faces and start sending more texts to safe, close friends that say, "Pray for me so I don't strangle my brother." Or maybe that's just me.

---

5   1 Samuel 18-20

I'm Good

My college dorm was not in good shape, to say the least. It was probably the sweetest and most tender home I will ever have, living with fifty girls who all loved Jesus and one another so sweetly, but oh were there spiders.

I personally don't really love animals; although, I've recently fallen in love with a cat I live with and I'm having a little bit of an identity crisis over it. That being said, above all animals, I hate insects more than any other creatures—and spiders the very most. They just look evil. And I feel as though they stare at me like, "Hey, I'm about to outrun you and hide forever and there is nothing you can do about it."

My dorm taught me all kinds of new things about spiders. I learned some could reach sizes I had never seen. I learned their bodies could be so big that when you stepped on them it left blood on your wall. I learned so much I wish I never did.

But one weekend, I learned more about spiders than ever before. Our window screens didn't quite meet our windows, and living in a dorm on top of a mountain about five miles away from civilization, these cracks in our windows were an open invitation to the party of the year for little spiders whenever it got cold outside. As it got colder, they would pour in those little cracks. I sprayed everything possible around the edges of our windows. We even taped the bigger holes, but still they managed to find a way in.

One morning, I woke up with an odd spot on my foot. It was on top of my right foot on a vein and kind of looked like carpet burn. I thought it was unusual, but I kept going. By that afternoon, it was swollen, hot, and freaking me out. I then began experiencing flu-like symptoms. I'm no doctor, but I knew something crazy was going on inside my body. I went to the student health center and then to a local clinic, where I learned my foot had been bitten by a brown recluse spider. I got an antibiotic and was told to rest and drink a lot of liquids.

I went to the grocery store to stock up on what I would need and what I felt like I could eat.

Weak, I carried my cases of water and groceries from the parking lot to my dorm and then up my stairs. I had to stop midway up the stairs because I was so weak. I felt light-headed and dizzy and like I could barely keep going, but I was determined to make it. So I did. "I'm good." I kept telling myself.

I spent the next four days in bed, watching *Friday Night Lights* and calling my mom in tears. The water and food I carried up my stairs with every ounce of energy I didn't have eventually ran out.

Before I could ask for help, a friend brought me soup and another made me bread. Countless friends fussed at me for not asking for help to carry my things inside. Friends came and lie in bed with me. Others helped me with my laundry and wrote me notes.

I've always wondered what it was like for the Woman at the Well to live such an isolated life. She had a less than respected reputation in her town, which caused the other women to look down on her and the men to only talk to her in secret. She had five husbands and came to the well at the heat of the day when it wouldn't be crowded, and she was probably hopelessly lonely. She was battered by the way her community had treated her, rough around the edges, and not cutting Jesus any slack. But He sat, saw, and spoke with her. He told her who she was and gave her Living Water.

What I love is that her transformation isn't just her own. She goes from her interaction with Jesus to tell everyone in the town, "See this man has told me everything I've ever done." Her whole town comes to follow Jesus because of her testimony.

See, there's a big difference in having friends who know who you are and friends you can call to carry water up the stairs for you. There's a big difference in friends who like your Facebook status or comment that they're praying for you, and friends who are with you on the darkest of nights. The same friend who brought me soup was the same friend a year later who sat and cried with me because I no longer had a daddy, after all the flowers had died and the cards stopped coming.

What did the Woman at the Well do when she was sick, and her family needed water? Who could she ask for help? She probably mustered up what energy she could and went to work.

That's the thing about pride. It isolates us.

Some of us are in situations where we truly don't have anyone. Most of us do have someone in our lives, but we are terrified to let them know we need them. We were raised to be strong, to focus on our responsibilities and battles, and to get the job done. No one tells us what to do when we can't.

I have a hard time knowing when I need anything, because this has been so engrained in me. I neglect my own needs—even eating and sleeping at times—because I get so caught up in meeting other's needs. (Yes, I am an Enneagram 2.) But when I'm desperate, empty, and at the end of my rope, I'm confronted with the needs I thought I had gotten rid of.

Because of my story, I have often given my needs a bad rap for making me "needy," "clingy," or "dramatic." The truth is, though, that our every desire—which leads to our needs—is given to us to bring us back to the feet of Jesus. Our desires for contentment, satisfaction, attention, and affection are not wrong. They are not weaknesses. Instead, they are means by which God reminds us that we are purposefully dependent. But we also have physical needs: clothes, shelter, and meals, for instance. We face these needs because we live in a world that is fallen from the Paradise that lacked no good and perfect thing we were created for. I believe these needs too are purposed to draw us back to the feet of Jesus. But they often do so by making us cross the path of His bride, the Church.

This past week was hard. It was exactly three months since Daddy's heart attack. I found myself sobbing, "God, how can you let this be this hard?" Later I found myself zapped of all energy. I had a hamper overflowing with more than a week's worth of laundry; I was worried about how I would pay for meals for the next few days because money was tight; and I truly just needed to be cared for. But that Sunday afternoon I lie in a bed in a house a very generous family let me live in for the summer, with clean sheets a friend had washed for me, having eaten a free lunch my church provided for me, and overwhelmed by the beauty of the body of Christ that even when I don't have the capacity to share my needs, God provides.

If ever there were a testament of the Body of Christ, it was when we were in the hospital fighting for my dad's life. When we weren't well. When I couldn't muster up the strength and courage to be fine. We were really broken and really needy. And we didn't go without one meal. There were always cookies, cases of water, gum, fruit, everything you could imagine. A sweet lady from church even made me a birthday cake and delivered it to my door.

If ever anyone was conditioned to say, "Oh, I'm good," when God places people in your path to care for you, it's me. But I have never been met in more real ways by Jesus than by being real with the people around me.

The disciples had a similar encounter. Following the crucifixion, they were lost and grieving and trying to figure out their new normal. So they were walking on the Emmaus road, talking about what they had experienced and being really broken with one another. On their journey, they came upon a stranger who asked them about what had happened. The story later reveals that this stranger was Jesus.

And no story paints the picture more clearly that Jesus meets us when we are real, raw, and broken with one another. We are all tired of mustering up our Sunday best to go to church and act like we have it all together, when inside we are barely holding on. For example, one Sunday I was at church for four hours and as I was leaving, a lady shared about the divorce she's walking through that will be finalized this week. The pain she shared on her face and through her tears was the most real conversation I had all morning.

This is where Jesus meets us. He meets us and draws us to one another as we are real with one another, allowing us to carry each other's burdens when we don't have the strength to carry our own.

Headaches, Pain, and Loneliness

Tonight I came home with a terrible headache. It was a very normal day. I had slept well, worked all day, went to dinner with a friend, and finished the evening at an event to hear one of my favorite speakers. I got home around 8:30. But this headache was sharp and demanded my attention. As the pressure in my right temple continued to impair me from functioning, this headache brought on a memory.

I had a few health problems in high school. There was a time when I dealt with some really bad headaches along with some other problems. One day my dad and I were in the grocery store and he, so attentive to me, was asking about my headaches. He paused and spoke in a serious tone.

"Now baby girl, when I was a little boy, I kept getting headaches for a little while. I remember a couple of times they were so bad I couldn't even speak. Everybody kept telling me I was making it up. I just want you to know if they are bad, that you can tell us, okay?"

I love that man.

While I've never had headaches so bad I couldn't speak, pain does have a similar effect. It isolates.

I've experienced this in ways before, but never so much in grief. I tend to always have an abundance of thoughts to share and rarely find it difficult to find words. I am growing in not finishing other people's sentences or interrupting them with my response to what I know they are about to say. I am highly verbal, and communication comes naturally to me, yet for the very first time when I was back on my college campus, staying at a cabin a week after my dad died, I felt what it was like for the very first time to not have words. I was with my friends Kate and Katie, who had been sweetly by my side day in and day out. I looked at them to describe the depths of pain I was experiencing, and no words came out. There weren't words I could associate with the pain in my head. It was just deep, wrong, and impossible to bear.

There is something about grief that is inherently isolating, but many other forms of emotional trauma have the same effect. In my Health Psychology class in college, we learned that one of the primary struggles patients with terminal or chronic illness report is loneliness and/or a lack of social support.

Tonight I attended an event at the college where I work to hear Sarah Bessey speak. It was incredible. Sarah shared about her four miscarriages and how broken she was to the point that she left the Church. "Sometimes we find ourselves in the company of unanswered prayers and that company doesn't always find itself at Church,[6]" she said.

Goodness, is that true. I remember sitting in countless church services following a week when I barely slept because I was so busy praying and hoping for my daddy's life, just to bury him a week later. Songs and phrases proclaiming "Nothing is impossible," "You heal all our disease," "You meet every need," "God is still in the business of performing miracles," "Seek and you shall find. Ask and it shall be given unto you," and worst of all, "You're a good, good Father," burned deeply in my bleeding heart. One night I sat through an entire service, hearing about miracles and healing and thought, *Has no one else here prayed for a miracle and didn't get the answer you wanted? No one else?*

And I think asking any question that begins with "Has no one else _____ ?" is exactly where the enemy would work to have us. Isolated, alone, doubting, questioning, and in pain. What a glorious position in his scheming eyes.

---

6   *Berry College Lumen Lecture.* By Sarah Bessey. Berry College, Mount Berry, GA, January 30, 2017.

Pain is a hard thing to invite someone into. There are not many encounters when it's easy to say, "Hi, can I tell you this really hard thing weighing heavy on my heart?" like the drive-thru line at Starbucks or the three-minute greeting at church. Just tonight, one of my spiritual mamas saw me and asked how I was doing, as we hadn't seen each other since about a week or so following my dad's death. "Okay," I responded. And then rehearsed over and over in my head how I should have sounded more excited or been more cheerful toward her. But if I'm real, I went home and cried angry, angry tears.

I think it's hard to let others into our hurt because most of the time they don't do it well, and often because they are afraid of hurt themselves. Like, imagine walking down the hall to the bathroom of your school or office and passing an acquaintance. "Hey, how are you?" you ask as a kind gesture. "Hurting," they respond, looking right into your eyes.

For most of us that would be a hard moment, or at least a little scary. If you then clarified they were hurting because they were sore from an intense workout the day before, that would alleviate some tension because we are a little more okay with physical pain. But if they were to share they were processing through past abuse, recently abandoned or betrayed in a relationship, or grieving a loved one, most of us quickly try to navigate how quickly and effortlessly we can get out of conversation with this person.

This is why we have paid professionals to walk people through processing their pain. Counseling is a blessed and sacred ministry that has met me in the deepest of places, but as the body of Christ, we mustn't only dismiss hurting people and encourage them to go to counseling. It is our job to mourn with those who mourn and weep with those who weep.

But mourning and weeping scare our Western minds that are so fixed on progress and improvement. We would rather enter into processing and coping because those sound more like accomplishing tasks.

I was terrified to enter into my own pain. I was scared of how people looked at me, terrified to say the wrong thing, many of them not saying anything at all. But I remember the people who asked me how I was and looked at me with stillness and care, then cried as I shared.

Often when people have asked, "Hey girl, how are you?" I've answered, "Good! How are you?" Because I feared they couldn't handle, "Actually, I'm just barely holding it together today and keeping my mascara in purse." Sometimes it is sacred to not let people into your pain so much. Sometimes they aren't safe enough and there is wisdom in knowing how much to share. But there is absolutely nothing sacred about constantly wondering, *Has no one else* _____? Because our Father knows what it's like to feel pain, to feel misunderstood, and to feel overlooked. He knows how to handle pain and wants to invite us to do exactly what my daddy pressed me to do—share it, knowing that we'll be met with care.

See the Mountains

I spent this past weekend in a cabin in the mountains of North Georgia with the college ministry staff I belong to. Our cabin was absolutely beautiful with the most stunning view. The whole back side of the house was lined with floor-to-ceiling windows, so we could sit and look out all day. My Instagram couldn't even capture the beauty. The blue, tree-covered mountains folded into one another for what seemed endless across the horizon. It was the kind of view that made you want to grow taller and taller just to see more of it.

The weekend was beautiful not only for the view, but for the incredible fellowship I had with the other staff. The main goal of our weekend was to share about where we were, what the previous year had taught us, and how we could pray for one another. Beautiful, right?

I listened to guys cry about hard transitions in their families, wives tear up about wishing their marriage could be more than circumstances permit, and friends share about how it's hard to know what next steps look like in planning their future when they'd always anticipated things different than they are. Real life stuff.

I was a ball of snot and tears as I shared the depths of how hard it was to let my dad go, how orphaned I feel, how lonely I feel, and how deeply I am wrestling with God. The others met me where I was, prayed for me, surrounded me, and blessed me.

One morning stuck out to me. My friend Jessica sat on the couch while she nursed her baby. My back was to the beautiful mountain view so I could face her. She had just lost her dad the summer before, following a few years of trauma and stress. Yet, being Jessica, she entered into my pain with me. As I shared the mess in my head, she shared truth. Honestly, I wasn't ready to receive it. I had to fight the anger and disbelief in my heart from showing up on my face, but I think what she did is exactly why we need community. She looked beyond me and saw the beauty.

As I sat in the shadows of the view of the mountains, I also sat in the darkness of my grief. And that darkness is real. It is hopeless and cold and lonely and terrifying. But when the people God puts in our lives come close, they can look beyond our shadow and see the grandeur of the view God is painting behind us, the folding tree-covered mountains, that only push us higher. And what my friend Stacie shared with me is, "You will never know true joy without allowing yourself to feel great pain." The best friends who walk through darkness with you are not ones who try to compartmentalize, categorize, and cover your pain.

I love the Jewish tradition of "sitting *Shiva*." It was customary that when a family member died, the family would sit in darkness in their home, on the lowest stool they owned. Family and friends would come for days, simply to sit in silence with them.

The day we took my dad off the ventilator, our friend and angel, Mrs. Gay, sat in silence with me. I don't remember much about that day, other than my heart burned with pain and that I laid my head on Mrs. Gay's shoulder. I don't know that she said a word all day. She gave me water and fended off people I didn't want to talk to.

Many of us have been scarred by friends who see the mountains for us when we could barely see three steps ahead in the valleys. I've learned this can be because we present ourselves as on top of the mountains when we really aren't, or because those friends haven't allowed themselves to be real enough to walk through their own valleys.

I think one of the best ways to see past someone's brokenness and believe the beauty beyond it is to just be there for them in their pain. To believe that no matter what they need space to do, you know that they are in the palms of Jesus' hands, and to speak it over them appropriately. And to help them know there is beauty on the other side of their grief, but it is okay to be real about how things seem from the depths of the valley. They seem empty, hopeless, exhausting, and dark. And one of the best ways to help them believe there is beauty when all they see are ashes is to just silently with them in the darkness.

The Heat of the Day

"It was about the sixth hour"[7] seems to be the one thing every Christian speaker knows to pull from the text of the Woman at the Well to prove their biblical knowledge. They explain how the woman went to get water at the hottest time of the day. Most people assume this is because she didn't want to be amongst the other women, because while the jar she carried to Jacob's Well was empty, it figuratively overflowed with the same thing many of us carry—shame.

---

7   John 4:6

I've learned a lot about shame this year. Some shame is often right and merited like shame that follows a murder, betrayal, or adultery. There is shame when you make a bad decision, or shame when it's discovered you aren't who you claim to be; but there is also unmerited shame. There are children who are shamed for being children, should they have needs or make mistakes their parents don't have time for. There are students who are shamed for not being better performers, when their minds don't work exactly the same as everyone around them. There are children with deformities who are shamed for looking or sounding different from others. There are individuals who are shamed for their size, poverty, gender, race, or whatever it may be.

The woman who went to the well, we assume, went at the hottest part of the day because somehow the sun's scorching rays felt less abrasive than the glares of the women in her community. She was the town harlot, the one whose name every man and woman knew. Her name was probably said in whispers and as brunts of the joke, and she didn't try to hide that the shame affected her. But she did try to escape it.

But while there is shame for mistakes we've made, there is often shame for things we never chose to carry. I have learned to identify and name many things I felt ashamed for in my childhood that, looking back, were very real experiences for a little girl.

And while shame seems like a small part of the human experience, I have found it to be the opposite. In the same way the Woman at the Well avoided every other woman by sweating to death to get the water she needed, shame motivates us. It tells us to start that diet, to text that guy we shouldn't, to go to the gym more, to stop telling people what's going on. Shame propels us.

Shame propelled me.

If I'm real, I was ashamed for a really long time for having any needs of my own. I hid behind the façade that I could be all things to all people. And for a long time, I was. I was a team leader at my Chick-fil-A in high school, an honors and AP student, a babysitter for a girl from church every afternoon, a leader in my church youth group, a volleyball player, a softball player, the student body vice president, a member of the yearbook and media team, and if you can't read between the lines, exhausted.

In college, I found myself in a similar situation. By my senior year, I was on staff with my college ministry, president of the Psychology honor society, a member of two other honor societies, a small group leader and worship leader at my church, a member of a group of bloggers, an occasional teacher for my college's English Second Language classes, a small group leader to college girls, and various things in between. Exhausted.

Exhausted, yet propelled by one little thing I had become aware of. Shame.

I was afraid of letting people see the real me. I was afraid of them ever seeing me as needy or inadequate, so if I was busy and in charge and in control, I could never be any of those things. And I was. I was busy and exhausted and in demand and absolutely empty on the inside. I was tired of eating lunch in my car as I ran from one thing to another. I was tired of all of my friends making plans and doing things and never inviting me because they thought I was too busy.

Shame motivated me. And for long enough it controlled me.

But this year, through a sweetly anointed Christian counselor, I was able to identify some of my key shame messages from my childhood, and it has been the most freeing thing of my entire life.

Is shame still a part of my life? Absolutely, but I have sat and looked my key people in the eyes and told them I was afraid if I didn't host them, help them, plan their parties, show up for them at the right times, and honestly just be a real human with them, that I wouldn't be enough. I was more scared than I could ever put words to of needing them. But I have learned to.

I've learned to text a friend when I am lonely and just need some company to do absolutely nothing.

I have learned to not be afraid to text a friend to go check if I turned my curling iron off because I can't stop thinking about it, even though it took a lot of guts for me to ask her to do it. (Love you, Ansley.)

Identifying my shame and learning to name and walk into it has totally changed how I see other people. People who weren't also driven to exhaustion made no sense to me. I assumed they were lazy or not good enough. But in learning to be real, I have been really loved and learned how to really see the value of people around me. The gift of friends with spare time to walk with me to the well and bear the heat of the day with me. The friends who over time have taken my jar of shame and replaced it with a jar of love, fullness, and freedom.

Airplanes and Abbie

I have never really been a big fan of airplanes. I was five years old the first time I ever flew, on my way to the happiest place on earth. That's right, Walt Disney World. At the time, we lived in southern Virginia, and the price of five plane tickets was overwhelmingly worth it to avoid a fourteen-hour-drive. I asked my Dad a million questions about what to do and how to behave on the plane because he traveled often for work.

We checked our luggage and made our way through security, which was much easier in the year 2000. When the moment came to walk down the ramp and on to the plane, my brain, true to its nature, decided to freak out. It realized I was leaving solid ground for the last time, and I was not okay with it. Sure, I loved Minnie Mouse, but I loved my life a lot more. I planted my two feet in my Barbie tennis shoes in the terminal and told my family I was not going. They, knowing I would cave in less than five seconds, looked at me and replied, "Okay, we'll see you next week." And kept on walking.

Planes have always terrified me. I love being able to travel and be more connected to the people and adventures that make this life so full, but you know that feeling. The one when the plane first takes off and you feel like it's climbing a roller coaster just before a big drop. Then, all of a sudden, your stomach drops and you can't breathe because it is going up and up quickly. Apparently, some of you crazy people love that feeling, like my friend Jenna does. I am the person sitting in her seat, surrendering her life to Jesus one last time, knowing I will soon see His face and wondering who I should leave all of my clothes to. (Jillian, Haven, Shelby, Carrie, and Lauren, feel free to share them all.)

It's a scary thing not to be in control, to give up the freedom to stop and pull over, or to turn around and go back. You're entombed in a large, metal tube darting through the skies, and you can only hope it was well engineered and maintained, and praying you make it back to the ground in one piece.

And just as much as these planes make life just as full as it is, relationships do the very same. Yes, romantic relationships take on this same form, but for me, this has meant friendships. And by friendships, I mostly mean my friend Abbie.

Abbie is a hard nut to crack. When I was a freshman in college and beginning to work with the student ministry at my church, I'd hear stories about "Abbie Brewster." I was not only determined to meet this girl, I was determined to be her friend. But because she was usually returning to her home in my college town at the same time I went back to my home for breaks, we didn't meet until a fall retreat in the mountains of Tennessee.

We've recounted this weekend more times than I can count. We were leading worship together, Abbie playing guitar and me singing. The best word to describe this weekend is *freezing*. Abbie really doesn't like being touched or asked deep questions or be talked to all that much, and if you know me you know those three things are me in a nutshell. But Abbie's shell was thick, and I handled trying to crack it open in all the wrong ways.

We were practicing for worship in about twelve degrees, and Abbie took her hands off her guitar and said, "I think my fingers are going to fall off, they are so cold." "Ooh! I can warm them up!" I responded, naturally seeing this as my door into friendship with her. (Side note: Like y'all, I really love people. Sometimes when my day isn't too busy, I will go to Starbucks and smile at people and hope they'll talk to me. I am that person.)

Abbie later told me that was the moment she knew we wouldn't be friends. Later that night when I was cold, she offered me a sweatshirt she later told me I wore for the next two days and never gave back. We kind of counted that weekend as a loss.

But the next year we led a Disciple Now together and for the first time really began to connect. I spent the following summer in Rome and we hung out at student ministry events occasionally. By the next year, we began leading worship together, practicing every Tuesday night and communicating regularly about songs. We became co-small group leaders and had dinner a few times to get to know each other ,and soon we were each other's other halves. Everyone around us still doesn't understand. Abbie hates shopping, loves dogs, likes to be left alone, hates being touched, and doesn't really like to talk about her feelings. And I'm Emily Katherine.

I found myself naturally prioritizing our friendship, seeking out dinner together at least once a week. All of my friends knew her, and the ones closest to me had spent significant time with her. We knew what was going on in each other's lives and soon what was going on with each other's hearts. Abbie has the rare gift of seeing right through people. She is one of those who seems to have a sign on her head at all times that reads, "Tell me your deepest, darkest secrets." In a world where I only let everyone else see the best and perfect me, Abbie saw the real me. She knew the mistakes I regretted. She knew who had deeply hurt me that I had never let show. She knew the fears I had covered with routines to get around them. She knew the boy I had a crush on who I shouldn't have. She knew the callings I felt afraid of.

Abbie shared more of her life with me than I ever imagined, and it always felt like such a joy and honor to be let in, because I knew I was joining a small crowd. I write this in past tense to describe the closeness and sacredness we shared before things reached an even deeper level.

The day I learned of my dad's heart attack, Abbie was one of the first people I told. I was supposed to lead worship at church with her that night and then teach small group, so I texted her to let her know I wouldn't be there and quickly told her why. She immediately called me and begged me to let her drive me to South Carolina, but I wouldn't. She had received a similar phone call in college that her mom had passed away, and she drove home alone. She knew what it was like and didn't want me doing it.

I didn't know how to be around anyone in that moment and I didn't want to wait any longer. I just needed to get to my daddy, so I didn't let her. What I didn't know until the next morning was that she, along with one of my other friends, Savannah, got in Abbie's car that same night and drove to Spartanburg. They stayed at a hotel in town without telling me, and then showed up with enough Chick-fil-A for a small country (courtesy of some of my Cathy friends I love so dearly) and said they were there for two days if I needed anything.

I was afraid of having anyone come with me because I was afraid of having to host them. I wasn't sure how long we would be in the hospital and I wasn't sure how to care for their needs along with my family, because I have never known how to let anyone care for mine, even though that's what Abbie and Savannah came to do.

Abbie came back for the funeral. She helped me move out of my dorm room and into my apartment. She washed every dish that came as a graduation gift. That whole summer, anytime she saw I was home, she was at the apartment. In one of the loneliest seasons of my life, I had to some days ask Abbie for space. She understood the loneliness of grief. She got that spending time with family was hard and the transitions of being with them to being alone were even harder. She bought me a cookie to celebrate the day my new planner began. She helped me move from my summer apartment into my home. She vacuumed and cleaned and came over just to spend time with me whenever. She saw me and cared.

Abbie taught me I could let people take care of me. I constantly told her on those move-in days how she didn't have to do anything for me. She could just sit and be there, but instead she would say, "Let me do this." She asked me questions about the hard things. I shared things with her I never shared with anyone.

Relationships are a lot scarier when you actually allow yourself to not be in control. It's kind of like the difference between driving and flying. There were lots of moments when I wanted to stop and pull over and reassess if the situation was safe. Sometimes I wanted to turn around and go back, but Abbie had become such a part of my life I never knew how to.

I just drove Abbie to Liberty University in Lynchburg, Virginia, to begin her Masters in Marriage and Family Therapy. I confidently drove a U-Haul trailer for ten hours, and I'm still really proud of that. We got her settled into her apartment, and my goodbye to her strikingly resembled Sandra Bullock's goodbye to her son in *The Blind Side*, before giving him a proper hug. Quick like a Band-Aid because I just couldn't do it.

I got on the plane to come back home, and was picked up at the airport for the first time by someone who isn't Abbie and it's just weird. I wept on the plane as I felt it doing the same thing my friendship with Abbie had. Taken off, feeling my heart race, getting past the first bumps and over the clouds, kind of wishing I could turn around and go back, but once we got above the clouds and I saw the setting sun I just kind of wanted to stay forever. I wasn't in control. It wasn't safe. But it was a view so beautiful I could only describe it, and that's what real relationships do. There aren't rest stops and gas stations, but there are views above the clouds that leave you speechless.

A Real Ministry

I remember the day that I realized I was called to ministry. I had thought it through and felt burdened to disciple young girls. I found myself at a conference in the old LifeWay Center in downtown Nashville, Tennessee, with three of the most influential women in my life, learning about girls' ministry, knowing this was what God had for me.

While I felt that call, I simultaneously felt *there's no way* and *I can't do this*. I still have those thoughts often. As my eleventh grade self sat in a session about caring for your heart well, I knew I needed to walk out, talk to my friend Jillian, and break up with the guy I was dating (because we don't all make the best decisions on dating at sixteen). I knew a lot of the plans I once had were now out the window, but I also knew that the one ahead of me was exciting and terrifyingly bigger than me. And it still is.

Ministry has taken on many forms for me. It began as a junior high camp counselor, a youth group volunteer, sixth grade tubing trip chaperone, high school choir tour chaperone, small group leader, and now college ministry staff member.

I have experienced countless moments that nothing in life can prepare you for. Like when I was on a trip full of seventh and eighth graders I had met only hours before, and was one of the only adults left when the others had to rush a student to the hospital. Or in the middle school girls' Bible study when we were reading the Psalm about how God "knew you in your mother's womb," and a seventh grader raised her hand to say she had eaten her twin in the womb. You can't make this up.

There have also been moments in ministry in which, I have been completely floored by the blessing it is to minister. As I see the faces of so many I love so deeply, treasuring the privilege have of a front row seat to their growth and transformation, I am overwhelmed with humility and gratitude.

But my unexpected experiences in ministry have only continued in learning I could love people in ways I never thought possible. The night my high school girls returned from their mission trip to Belize and came over to my apartment to eat cookies and play Catch Phrase, brought way too much joy to my heart. As we were all screaming answers at the top of our lungs, I looked around and breathed it in—this moment I had prayed for since I was 16—to have girls come to my house and get to love and be with them.

Last week I sat on my couch in my living room and cried with my friend Chelsea, telling her how much I loved her and how much she meant to me.

I love receiving texts such as, "Can I come cry at your house?" "Okay, EmK, I have a life question." "Can I have a futon shipped to your house?" and, "Can I come look through your closet tomorrow?" (By the way, I received all of these today!)

There are countless students, many of which are only about two years younger than me, who call me Mom, and few things in life bring me greater joy.

But amidst this joy, there is a sense in which this calling is utterly terrifying.

Remember when someone wanted to follow Jesus and he said, "Hold on; let me go bury my father." And Jesus responded, "Let the dead bury the dead."

Remember when Paul stopped persecuting Christians, was blinded into a place of following Jesus, and was then imprisoned.

Remember when Stephen testified of Jesus and was stoned for it.

Remember when the Woman at the Well's life was changed by Jesus and she had to go through town telling everyone, "He told me everything I'd ever done!" Knowing the whole town knew exactly what that meant.

Jesus calls us to do some crazy stuff. And sometimes it is absolutely exhilarating. I was terrified to board the plane, but loved every minute of working with students in Brazil to translate one of Chick-fil-A's leadership books to be relevant in a tribal culture. There have been few sweeter days in my life than the day I flew to Oklahoma to help lead worship and teach two breakouts at one of the first events for women at my friend Jillian's church in Oklahoma. I have loved sitting under people like Bob Goff, author of *Love Does*, whose crazy adventures to love people in order to make Jesus' name famous never cease to amaze me and keep me laughing.

But there are moments in ministry that are hard and scary. There are hard conversations with students, parents, friends, supervisors, pastors, and Jesus. There are moments when I feel like the Woman at the Well as God calls me to share pieces of my story that I am ashamed of, but know He is overwhelmingly able to redeem.

And there are moments when I feel like I flat out don't have it in me. Like last week when I was working at a conference two hours away and had to travel back on Wednesday night. I listened to the song I was supposed to sing at church that night on repeat and called a friend to send me a picture of the lesson I hadn't read. Or today when I was driving to pick up a student for lunch and said, "Jesus, I really don't have it in me, so you have to do this."

And there are days when I crave something a little safer. Like, I wonder what it was like for Matthew the tax collector to leave his established, safe, and secure job to follow Jesus, not knowing where they would sleep each night and if they would have enough food to eat. My sacrifice pales in comparison to Matthew's and especially to Jesus, but if I'm real, I love safe. I am that person who pays each bill within twenty-four hours because I'm scared I'll forget. I get oil changes as soon as they are due so nothing will happen to my car. I have routines for flossing, cleaning my coffee maker, replacing the baking soda in the refrigerator to keep it fresh, and getting annual physicals, yet I am called to a career that is anything but safe and predictable—especially for a female.

I came from a businessman and a nurse who were first-generation college students. Their parents: manufacturing employees at Budweiser, automotive parts providers, and blood donation center clerks. Safe, dependable, predictable.

What even is the ministry I'm called to? I make myself write it down pretty often because I often guilt myself into thinking I'm falling ridiculously short.

The ministry I am called to first and foremost is to "follow." To go where He goes, love how He loves, serve how He serves. What a blessing that calling has no gender.

But following doesn't necessarily come with benefits, retirement, insurance, or free child care (you know, for all my children). And I crave safe. I crave settled and rooted and predictable, but I don't think that's what ministry is. Sometimes it is. It is a deep and meaningful calling to be the constancy in students' lives when everyone else has failed to be.

But for me, it means taking risks, like finishing this book that may go nowhere. Ministry means sacrifice. It means giving and going, even when it's not what serves you best. The most real ministry for me has been the most sacred ministry.

The least safe ministry has been inviting the students whose lives I get to be a part of to see my brokenness. It felt wrong at first. I wondered how in the world I could look at an eighteen-year-old and say, "Hey I'm walking through grief and kind of really falling apart, but I'm so excited to be a part of your life. Please let me be here for you."

Those weren't my words, but that was the song of my heart. I had to learn to say no some days. Some days I couldn't get coffee. Some days I didn't respond to texts, and my counselor would proudly tell you that was repentance for me (thanks, Heather). Some days I cried in staff meetings and some days I decided to not be all things to all people and be quiet in a circle of girls where I felt pressured to be the one asking all of the questions.

And the most meaningful ministry has taken place for me when I have allowed others into my sacred. Not into just the safe parts of ministry for me, such as asking how they are and sharing what books we are both reading, but the sticky parts. Like crying with a student who just ended a really long and meaningful relationship, because I know what it's like to lose the person who sees and knows you best. Like telling a student that I get what it's like to have incredible parents who you want to be so thankful for, yet there are parts you need to process because you feel the weight of them. And gently nudging the strongest of friends to be okay with being delicate and broken in a hard season. That there is strength in that, when delicacy has been so shamed in a culture that devalues women.

Moments of unsafe conversations have been the most transformative, yet the most difficult. Like telling a student how I had always known her as kind, gentle, and thoughtful, yet she was currently coming off as hard to get along with. Telling a student she couldn't go to a Christian conference one weekend, because I knew she wasn't in the right place for it, and telling a student that if she kept living the way she was she would continue wasting her potential.

But there's something about the unsafe. It's like when Peter stepped out of the boat onto the water. There is delicate balance at stake. There is an infinite need to keep my eyes deeply fixated on Jesus. And there is much room to quickly slip. Yet, there is much growth in stepping out of the boat, not just in learning from that experience, but in the trust and the depth that is forged from that very fixation on Jesus' eyes.

REAL SAVIOR

Wave After Wave

The beach is one of my favorite places. Growing up, we would go on vacation to the beach with family friends every summer. I went through a long phase of being more of a pool girl, but I've come back around to my first love—the ocean. I love how big it is, how mysterious it is, how there's so much life inside of it, how connected it makes me feel to the rest of the world, how it makes my hair look later in the day, everything. My mom, a fellow beach lover, taught me the art of ocean swimming. I mean, it's not anything novel, but what we love is to get to the part of the ocean where the waves haven't folded over yet. I'm sure there's a smart biology term for this, but you know what I'm talking about. The kind of calm area where you can still touch, just past where the waves are crashing. I love it! Even as I'm typing this, I can imagine myself bobbing around in the waves. It's one of my favorite feelings.

The summer after my dad passed away, my family spent a week at the beach together. Each day, I'd walk into the ocean once I had let myself work on my tan enough, and I made infinite connections between the ocean and my grieving. I'd even dare to say that these connections may be true of any hard thing in our life we have to work through—a break up, sexual abuse, divorce, pornography addiction, however the brokenness takes form.

I love so much to get to the calm part, beyond where the waves crash, but to get there I must be hit by wave after wave. Sometimes they are painful, like *where in the world did all of that power come from*? Sometimes they knock me over in the process. And I almost always reach a point as I'm going to swim in the ocean when I think I'll just turn back because I hate walking through the part where the waves crash into me so much.

But I know it's worth the crashing to get past it, so I keep going. I get knocked down, then blink to clear the salt water from my eyes. Sometimes my bathing suit bottoms fall down, and I pray no one is standing close by.

Sometimes the waves look bigger than they are and end up being much more gentle than expected, and sometimes they look gentle and end up knocking the breath out of me. I think it's the unexpected ones that are the hardest.

The pain of losing my dad sucks. It hurts like salt in the deepest of wounds. Every single day I must remind myself its real because it feels so wrong and unnatural. But something inside of me knows that on the other side of these waves of pain that knock me over, surprise me, and make me want to give up, there's peace. That as much as the process is slow and hard, I can only go through it to get to the other side.

We weren't made for pain. We weren't made for needs. This thought blows my mind. When Adam and Eve lived in the garden of Eden, every single one of their needs were met in Him. They had no other needs and lived in a world with no pain.

This past year, one of my best friends had the most beautiful baby girl. She is named with my same initials, so I knew from the moment I heard Jillian was having her that our souls were connected. Baby Eliza Kate actually waited for me to get to the hospital (over a week her mom did not love!) all the way in Oklahoma before she made her grand appearance. Gosh, I love that little nugget.

I spent the whole first week of Eliza Kate's life with her and her parents, Jillian and James, and just died over how much I loved her all week long. One thing that I had never thought about before was watching Eliza Kate eat. Never before the day she was born had she ever felt hunger. She was probably crying because she had never even felt pain before, and the faint feelings of hunger was the most need she had ever been in. And as she ate, she began to have gas, because that's what babies do. And the pressure of gas in her little digestive system was the most pain she had ever felt before. She was having to learn to feel the needs and pains of this broken world that we are more familiar with.

If I'm real with you, as I have walked into these salty, strong waves, I have only wanted to go back. I've wanted to give up and stop feeling the pain. I have cried. I have ugly cried because just like Eliza Kate had every need met before she was born, I was meant to have every need met and none of this pain. And I haven't been able to form any eloquent words while praying. Many times my prayers are a lot more like those "groanings too deep for words" that the Holy Spirit intercedes for us with, according to Romans 8:26-27 (English Standard Version).

But the journey of learning how to stand on your own two feet and walk into the ocean is one that takes practice and strength.

When I was little, I always wanted to swim in the ocean because that's where my brothers were, so that's exactly where I wanted to be. I would tell my parents, "I want to go swim!" and they would tell me, "Okay, go sit on the edge." Like I was ever going to be pleased with that.

Then my daddy would come and pick me up and carry me into the ocean. He took the brunt of the waves because he knew I wasn't strong enough to handle them yet. And when they came, he would pull me in tight to keep me safe and keep me from getting scared. And after each one came and he showed me he had me, we went further. I kept asking him if he could touch and making him promise he was telling the truth. Sometimes, when we got deep enough and a big wave came, he would lift me up over it. Then, we would get to the smooth part I love, letting each gentle little wave lift us up and set us back down.

And while I have tears in my eyes as I'm typing this, I think walking back into our hurt is impossible sometimes. It just hurts too bad. The burning I feel in my chest when my heart breaks from missing my daddy begins to come back, because we weren't created for this brokenness and these needs. And we face our pain like newborns.

We don't have a concept or instincts for grieving and pain. Instead, we have to know we aren't big enough or practiced enough. Early on, the waves are too big for us. And I think that somehow, we have to let our Heavenly Father come and pick us up and walk with us into our hurt. As wave after wave crashes, let Him take the brunt. Let your prayers be groanings, feel the salt in all of your wounds, and let Him squeeze you in tightly. And as you go deeper, it's okay to ask Him if He's big enough or if He's trustworthy.

The Psalmist would repeatedly ask questions to the extent of, "Are you just going to leave me here to die?"[8] I think we can ask Him to prove Himself. And when the waves are bigger than we can handle, He has to lift us up. We don't have the strength. We weren't meant for this.

But I think there's a big qualifier here in that I knew I could trust my dad. He was so careful to always honor me that he even asked my mom if it was appropriate for him to change my diaper. And sometimes when we're walking into this pain or brokenness in our lives, our Heavenly Father is the very one we blame for it.

And I am learning to be real in that anger.

I love nothing more than stories in the Bible of people who were straight up raw with God, like Hannah weeping at an altar because she couldn't have a son, so much that the priest thought she was drunk[9], or Hezekiah so angry that he was going to die that he just stared at a wall because he was so distraught.[10] I have wept and I have stared at walls and I have asked God why and I haven't gotten an answer. And so many people have told me to just choose to believe things. Please don't do that. Please do not take the road of putting a band-aid over a wound that needs stitches. It will only bleed through.

Instead, I have had to sit on the beach with God and ask Him *how?* And *why?* And I know part of it comes back to

---

8   Psalm 22
9   1 Samuel 1
10   Isaiah 38:2

Adam and Eve and the broken world we live in, that death and hurt and heartache are naturally a part of, but I feel in my every cell that this isn't right. I feel like Eliza Kate who would scream at the top of her lungs because her little belly was in so much pain as I'm screaming, "No! I can't handle this! I wasn't made for this!"

And I can't tie walking into our darkest, most painful hurts neatly with any platitudes, because if you have walked into it at all you know that you kind of want to punch the people who throw cute clichés at you. But what I can tell you are the lyrics to a song the Lord has put on my heart to a song I love that we find Him as we seek Him. And as we grow to love Him more, we learn how little we need any other thing.[11]

So I pray we let Him prove that He's trustworthy every step of the way. And I pray that we let ourselves feel the fear and pain every step of the way. But most of all, I pray that you walk square into those crashing waves, because you know the peace on the other side is worth fighting for. Let Him carry you there.

11 Jordan, Leslie, Leonard, David, Garrard, Stu, and Mabury, Paul. (2013). Integrity Music. *Oh How I Need You.*

Broken Hair

Hair is a teacher. Well, at least it is for me. Hair is a teacher and also a thermometer that measures how I'm actually doing.

I learned in the summer of 2016 that hair essentially serves as the body's filter. I learned this as a result of losing significant amounts of hair due to the trauma of losing my dad. The loss continued and worsened while the ends became even more dead and dry, feeling all too similar to everything else in my world. I was frustrated by this new loss and desperate for all forms of deep conditioning treatments, yet what I did not prepare for was the new hair that grew to replace the hair I lost. Hair that due to its newness was much shorter than the rest of my hair.

I recently read the passage in 2 Samuel 6 about how David commands the ark of the covenant's transportation to Jerusalem. He instructs the men transporting the ark to use a cart rather than the rods designed for carrying that God commanded them to use. In transit, the cart began to fall. Uzzah, seeking to protect the very object that carried God's immense glory, reached to keep the ark from falling and steadied it with his hand. Upon touching the ark of the covenant, Uzzah immediately died.

I remember reading this passage when I was younger and was struck by how strange the story seemed to me. Was Uzzah not seeking to be obedient, and even helpful? Why in the world did he die? This passage was assigned reading for a Bible class I took growing up, which led to a mind full of questions. I walked across the hall to my brother Michael's room, puzzled. When I asked him about the passage, he responded, "That's literally one of the hardest passages in the Bible for me to wrap my mind around. I just cannot seem to fit that together with God's nature."

But Uzzah's life did not end as a consequence of his behavior necessarily; rather, he died because of the glory of God.

The glory of the God of Abraham, Isaac, and Jacob, the God who led the Israelites on dry land across the Red Sea; the God who led the Israelites through the wilderness with a pillar of cloud by day and a pillar of fire by night, providing for them exactly the food they needed each and every day. The immensity of the glory of this God could not be touched by human hands. And if David and these men could successfully carry the ark on a cart to Jerusalem, they would have overlooked the need to carry the ark as God prescribed. His plan of how the ark was to be transported as His glory and presence rested with His chosen people, was through rods on their shoulders, traveling in the center of the Israelites. When they traveled throughout the wilderness, the ark would go before and be in the center of their midst as it rested on these rods.

Where am I going with this? I often do not feel capable of carrying God's glory. Especially now. This week I sat in a room with thirty-two students whose precious lives I desperately desire to be a crucial part of, but just like my hair, there are parts of me that feel dry and broken, along with new areas of growth that feel too weak and short.

So why, God? Why would you not just choose, but *demand* that your glory rest on me? Rest on us? Rest on each of your children? What little understanding I have grasped has taught me that He delights in dependency, knowing that this begins with brokenness. Making use of a cart provides a surefire way of carrying a big, important box from one place to another. A girl who has everything together is most likely capable of investing in the lives of thirty-two college students.

But tired people with rods on their shoulders have to depend both on one another and on God for their strength to keep the ark from falling and to continue moving forward. And I have to press into Him with every fiber of my being.

Pressing into the "Lord of Hosts." The Message describes this name of God as the God who is "at the end of our rope."[12]

So I'm learning to deep condition my hair and pull it up halfway. I am learning to press into Jesus to somehow transport His glory to the people I love and feel called to. And nothing is more on the forefront of my mind, surrounded by broken and new hair, that "apart from Him I can do nothing."[13]

---

12 Matthew 5:3
13 John 15

Bones

Bones are such a weird thing. Yes, they hold up our bodies and have a specific biological make up, but the ways we reference them are so interesting. To know something in your bones seems to carry more depth than your mind or heart. Sometimes it even feels more trustworthy than your soul.

I've heard the verse over again in my head, "Let the bones that you have broken rejoice."[14] I love the Psalmist's realness and brokenness over his sin. He doesn't ignore the pain and the hurt and tell himself that he should submit or believe.

---

14 Psalm 51:8

David doesn't tell himself that a king wouldn't have these thoughts, these wrestlings, or these hurts. Instead, he brings the depths of the pain to God.

I had a hard time putting words to my hurt in the first months of grief, but this verse resonated with me deeply. I do feel like these are bones that He has broken. Bones that were originally gifts from Him. Bones that were intended to be a part of the core of who I am. Bones that I depended on. Broken. And the new ways of walking and moving and living are awkward and tiresome and painful.

I have deeply resonated with the story of Mary and Martha when Lazarus dies. In fact, while we were in the hospital with my dad, that story constantly came to my mind. I repeated, "This sickness will not end in death,"[15] over my dad. This week, my boss shared in staff devotions about how we gloss over the story of the hurt and agony Mary and Martha faced while pleading Jesus to heal Lazarus.

But Mary and Martha knew in their bones Lazarus was going to die. They knew in their bones Jesus could heal him. And when He didn't come and when Lazarus died, they knew in their bones it was wrong. They were hurt, grieving, and devastated. And when Jesus finally came a few days later, Martha went rushing to meet Him and to tell Him just how much He had let them down, but Mary stayed.

I feel like Martha gets me. I would be the busy one in the kitchen. I would be telling Jesus how He should actually

---

15   John 11:4

do His job. But Mary stayed. Mary stayed in her home with all the people who had come to grieve with her family in Bethany. Mary was grieving and probably didn't feel like talking to Jesus. But He called her to Him.

And for once in this season of life, I've felt like Mary. I have pushed Jesus as far back as I can because every fiber of my faith that has always been good and easy to believe has now found a sharp point on the other end that cuts deeper and deeper into my pain. He's good. He's faithful. He fulfills His promises. He works all things together for good. My weak and frail bones can't bear the weight.

What we later learn is that Jesus heals Lazarus from the dead. And we know that even later, Mary washes Jesus' feet with her hair. But I still feel like the Mary who stays back to grieve with all the people sitting in silence. How does she reach the point, though some time passes, of worshipping Jesus by pouring out perfume at his feet?

What my friend Jeremy pointed out this week is that Mary reached a point of worshipping Jesus in such a broken, intimate, and sincere way because she had stewarded disappointment well.

And I believe when we think of stewarding disappointment well, we think of telling ourselves to suck it up or looking at the positives. But this isn't a disappointment of walking to the freezer and discovering we are out of ice cream, or waking up to discover it's raining. This is a disappointment that we feel in our bones. A disappointment that breaks us deeply inside. A disappointment and a brokenness in which God calls us directly to Himself—broken, doubting, and frail.

Psalm 51 is a psalm of David's brokenness over his sin. He says, "You delight in truth in my innermost being." And, "My only sacrifice acceptable to God is a broken spirit." He is deeply broken over his sin. He feels the weight of it deep in his bones. So how do broken bones rejoice? I think they start by feeling pain. The break is sudden and traumatizing and painful.

Jesus is not afraid to sit with us in our brokenness. He doesn't always fix it, I know from experience. But He sits with us, as He sat with Job when he suffered so much. He sits with us like a parent when we're sick, knowing they've done all they can do to help us, but the illness has to run its course. Yes, if He willed He could heal us, but sometimes we just have to endure. But you don't always have to trust He knows best in the process. It's okay to ask Him to prove it. And we have to know deep within our bones that brokenness is the first step to new growth and new life.

In the hospital, my sister-in-law Katherine read us a poem by Elisabeth Elliot. It was about how in order for a pine tree to grow, the acorn has to die. It goes down into the earth and loses its shell. And after a dark and hard process, soon a pine tree begins to grow.

Brokenness will lead us to a lot of places, but it cannot lead us to inauthenticity. Yes, it can lead us to coping mechanisms or ways to hide our inadequacy, but ultimately it leads us to the truest version of who we really are. It removes our masks, strips us of our strength, and makes us dependent.

Gill's Exposition of the Entire Bible comments on Psalm 51:8, saying,

For though the love and favour of God cannot be lost, yet his sensible presence, which puts joy and gladness into the heart, may; and though an interest in Christ ever continues, and union to him is always the same; yet a view of interest in him, which fills with joy unspeakable and full of glory, and communion with him, may not be had for a time: and though justification by his righteousness, from whence flows much peace, is an invariable blessing; yet the comfortable perception of it may be taken away: and though salvation by Christ is a certain thing, yet the joy of it may be lost for a season; which was now the case of the psalmist.[16]

The season of death, emptiness, and loss is dark, lonely, and hopeless. And our perception that is our reality of that darkness is an okay place to invite Jesus into. He's faced His own dark realities. He can't meet us in the realities we ourselves are seeking to escape; He meets us there by drawing us to them. Which often includes broken bones.

16   John Gill, *John Gill's Exposition on the Entire Bible-Book of Psalms*, 2nd ed. (Dallas: Graceworks Multimedia, 2011).

A Real Calling

H ave you ever seen a movie in which two different realities take place? I'm thinking of *Stranger than Fiction* and *Groundhog Day*, or more recently *La La Land*, a musical featuring Ryan Gosling and Emma Stone. When the movie ends to the audience's surprise, it revisits the alternative and what it would have taken for the conclusion to be different, or why the conclusion the audience wanted wasn't what they got. There was the reality they were in and the reality that could have been, and sometimes I see life that way. And by sometimes I mean right now.

I am currently sitting in the bookstore at Liberty University in Lynchburg, Virginia. I can see the whole reality that was meant to be my life here, and yet knowing it wasn't. See, I grew up in a little town called Danville, Virginia, just forty-five minutes down the road. From my first days I was taught a few things: go to church, love Jesus, honor your parents, drink your milk, and do everything possible to go to Liberty.

This may seem minor in the details of a happy childhood that I see looking back. But it wasn't. I couldn't just memorize my Bible verses for AWANA (a Bible memorization program) each week and get my AWANA dollars to go to the AWANA store and buy strawberry Laffy Taffy that I made sure to eat before going to get ice cream after church with my dad every Wednesday night. No, no. That wasn't good enough. I had to get the "Timothy Award," which was basically the student of the year award because despite the fact that I was only in third grade, it later counted as a scholarship to Liberty.

There were mission trips for which any money you spent could later be used to buy Liberty textbooks and church camps where students competed for prized scholarships provided in coveted orange envelopes. Sunday night services often enlisted Liberty students or graduates as guest speakers, and the only sure thing that was ever told to me about my destiny was Liberty University.

I don't want to downplay the incredible experience Liberty could have been for me. So many influential people, even in my own story, have stepped onto this campus, gazing at the beautiful mountains, and been transformed into notable leaders in the kingdom of God. But that wasn't God's plan for me.

So I sit here in this reality of the present and the possible. Looking at the mountain with its giant LU, and thinking how different things would have been. Who would I have met here? Who would I have never known? What job would I have had here? What opportunities would I have missed?

This could have been my world, my life, my home. But it isn't, and I'm thankful for the one God had for me instead. The one in which He has broken me and shaken me to my very core to teach me that what I believed to be the gospel was really just an idea that I had to keep striving. That what I thought was community was really just inviting people to know my best representative. And that what I thought was my calling was actually deceptive, considering the purpose and worth He has sung over my life.

But experiencing the *could have been*s are always a little weird. Sometimes they bring much thankfulness, like seeing the guy who could have been my world, and being thankful he is married to someone else. But sometimes it means seeing a girl out hiking with her dad and wishing I were her.

I spent the last week in Washington, DC, coaching students in the WinShape College Program how to discover their life purpose, and I absolutely loved it. In this program, our students spend time thinking through their stories and lives. They process their own gifts, talents, abilities, and interests. They think through what energizes them, what they lose time doing, what makes them really angry, and what they would give their life for to see changed in the world. From this, they write a one-sentence "Life Purpose Statement."

I've learned it is a rare thing to take the pen of the story of your life in your own hands. To sit in the grey areas of what could have been and what is. And sometimes the most beautiful growth you can have in your walk with Jesus is to be really angry with God about that.

I have sat with students who have looked at me and bravely said words such as, "I struggle with same-sex attraction and I have been ashamed of it my whole life." "I am addicted to pornography." "I have honestly never felt like my parent loved me." "I was sexually abused by my boyfriend." "My dad was never emotionally available to me."

The chills and tears return as I write those words, although what I know is that for a long time, I believed my calling was to know the broken parts of my story, but trust and glorify God anyway. To go and make disciples of all nations, but totally forget that there are dark and hidden parts of my heart that scream, "I don't know if this is real! How are you a good Father when you didn't _____!"

Seeing little girls look up at their daddies and giggle has brought this feeling up more than ever. I see the *could have beens* of the day I am given away as a bride to the love of my life, and how I always imagined looking back to see a tear in my dad's g big eyes, and knowing I never will.

Many people have told me to "choose joy." Many have lovingly said things such as, "God has a reason," and, "He works all things together for good." If I am honest, those statements have made me want to run away from any faith at all more than anything else. Choosing to believe God is good when the wound and hurt in my heart is open, gaping, and bleeding uncontrollably led me to moments of telling God I just couldn't do it anymore. I couldn't have faith. I couldn't believe that He is good. Those statements led me to moments of sitting in Bible studies and wondering what my calling would be if it weren't ministry.

The truth is I have learned my calling has never been and never will be choosing to believe anything. I think Taylor Swift describes this well, explaining the deep wounds formed cannot simply be covered by a Band-Aid.[17]

In his book *To be Told*, Dan Allender writes that often times when the hard and raw parts of our stories surface, we begin to "stamp truth" on them to cover them up. I felt this the most the day of my sweet daddy's funeral. I stood in the same sanctuary where I was baptized, as hundreds of people formed a line to greet and hug us. Hundreds. Black, white, young, old. Hundreds. All whose lives my daddy had touched. So many of them were so kind and generous to travel extensively to be there for us.

---

17   Swift, Taylor, Lamar, Kendrick, Martin, Max, and Shellback. (2015). Big Machine Nashville. Bad Blood.

However, a dear friend told me before the funeral to prepare myself to hear some of the most hurtful and minimizing words during that hour and a half, and I realized he was right when I heard the words, "You are doing so good to be so strong." "Just keep on taking care of your Mama." "Keep your chin up, girl." And as I have somehow entered into this unspoken club of other friends who have lost parents, they shared similar experiences of relatives saying, "Well, you are sure to meet some cute boys at the funeral!"

I could jump on my soap box about the worst things to say to someone who has lost a loved one, but the truth is we are uncomfortable with pain and want to make it go away immediately. So in the Church, we cover it with truth, no matter how inapplicable or cliché it may be, because actually walking square into the pain and hurt seems far too hard. What I've learned is that a life of holding to a cliché hurts all the worse.

I, along with fellow hurting friends, have walked through our stories and been angry at God, hurt by Him, and real with Him about our *could have been*s that we have grieved. As we laid clichés and cover ups, coping mechanisms and addictions, and even lies that this is what we deserved at His feet, we have come to find our very calling.

We have felt the deep healing we never thought possible when we are real, raw, and honest with God. And as our good Father, He does not need our protecting. He meets us at the end of ourselves and speaks to our hurts. When we stop choosing clichés and start choosing the gospel, we learn that the gospel doesn't mean choosing anything. It means accepting what has already been done for us.

Walking with God through our realities and *could have been*s brings a healing and wholeness that drives us to embody transformation and nudge those around us to it as well. When you see the reason why your reality is not what you wanted and why it had to be that way, you want everyone else to have that clarity too.

I haven't learned why my dad died. And I never will. But I have learned to name and invite God into my own brokenness in ways I never knew possible.

There is calling on the other side of healing, but often our calling is that very thing. Healing.

When Jesus met the Woman at the Well, He didn't tell her to forget her story. He never disregarded her past and told her who she was didn't matter. No. When she went to tell the whole town about Jesus, she was sure to include, "He told me everything I've ever done."

"Go and call your husband," Jesus told her. At first, I was caught by the sharpness of those words. They felt shaming. But as I read more, what I found was Jesus whispering her calling to dig deeply into the hurt in her life that she was living out through countless unhealthy relationships with men. He was inviting her to wrestle with her own brokenness just as Jacob, whose well they met at, had wrestled with God himself.

A Real Salvation

"Everyone wants the benefits of the cross, but very few want to receive the way of the cross." My mentor said these words to me yesterday that keep echoing in my mind.

I've said both last week and this one that I almost feel these weeks have been competing with themselves on how they can get any harder. I've been reading 2 Corinthians 4 over and over claiming, "I am pierced but not crushed, persecuted not abandoned, struck down but not destroyed." But if I'm real, I *have* felt crushed, abandoned, destroyed, hard pressed on every side to even believe that God is good.

That He loves me. Or that He has good things for me. We all want the benefits. And I do the very most.

I want His kindness, goodness, faithfulness, gentleness. I want to be covered in His righteousness that I could never deserve. I want to go to Heaven. I want to know my dad is with Jesus.

But I sure as heck don't want this. I would very easily trade it all—everything I've learned, every way I've grown, every pattern of thinking that has been stripped raw and bare to have "home" back again. Home in my daddy's sweet embrace. I loved the way he would hold me and squeeze me tightly into his big chest. "See, this is where you belong," he would always affirm. Home with my parents being my parents. This is a part of the grief journey no one prepared me for, that in a way when you lose one parent you lose two.

I'm blessed to have two parents who had been together and in love since they were nineteen years old. It was hard to identify where one stopped and the other began. They had an eerily similar sense of humor, passion to serve people, and drive to live life to the fullest, no matter the limitations in front of them. They equally empowered each other, believed in one another, sacrificed for one another, and when necessary, served as a safe place for one another. And when I lost my daddy, I lost my mama as I knew her. Without him, she wasn't her, and I think this is what true love does. A love like Johnny and June.

I miss home in the sense of predictability. Every time I went home for a weekend from college, we would go out for dinner on Friday, typically at the Fish Camp (a seafood restaurant in upstate South Carolina where your food is served on big metal trays and every waitress knows your name and your order). After that, my mom would go home and fall asleep early on the couch while my dad and I would go see a movie. He always got popcorn and layered on the butter. He would cry during the movie and I would psychoanalyze the characters and create care plans for their mental health in the car on the way back home. He would laugh at me.

On Saturday, we would sleep in and my dad would go get chicken biscuits from Chick-fil-A that would be in the microwave when I woke up. My mom would have made coffee. They would probably be out in the yard doing some type of work and I would hunt all over to find them. We would go to lunch together and my mom and I would go shopping while my dad changed the oil in my car and washed it. We would meet for dinner together and then I would go home to start the homework I'd been putting off all weekend, while watching a movie on TV with my dad.

On Sunday, we would go to church. Typically, my dad was running sound and my mom and I would sit together. Then, he would wait for us to talk to everyone we knew before going to stand in line at my favorite home-cooking restaurant for Sunday lunch. When we got home, my Mom would help me gather my things and all the laundry she had done for me, while my dad went to fill my car with gas. They would stand in the driveway and wave as I drove off. It was normal and predictable and seemed like a part of life that would always be there. Until it wasn't.

I miss home in the sense of being seen and in the sense of always having a place to depend on. I've often said that I feel like one day I was twenty-one and the next I was an adult, as my dad passed on the day I turned twenty-two. Actually, the exact minute. What a weird thing. As I am writing this, ten months have gone by since he passed and I still think to call him all the time, whether about what to do in my professional life or the tire pressure light that's been on my dashboard for about four of those months. (For the record, I've filled the tire with air many times.) But now is time to be a big girl. The house I lived in with my family is now a place where I contribute to big person decisions, where I've called to make life insurance claims, where I need to go and get the box of my childhood things, because my mom is moving in with my grandparents soon.

We moved when I was in sixth grade from a tiny town where most people felt comfortable disciplining me because they all knew my parents—and I probably needed it. All our extended family lived around the corner from each other until a moving truck took us three hours away from any family or anyone we had ever known. But we found a church. This church surrounded us and blessed us overwhelmingly. This is the church where I was called to ministry, baptized, and where I was given the mentors and people who made me who I am.

When we were in the hospital with my dad, this family God gave us was there for every hard moment. When my daddy lie in the ER without a pulse, every minister was there with my mom praying for one, when my dad suddenly wiggled his toes. They brought us every meal and every thing you could imagine in between. They sat with us to pass the time. They lie on the floor with me at the moment he died and asked me about my favorite memories of him. They cleaned our house to prepare for everyone coming over. They have blessed us tremendously.

But this sense of home has kind of been shattered for me. It's like a game of Jenga where each block has been carefully and perfectly stacked, but when you pull a certain block, everything comes tumbling down. That block was the breath in my daddy's lungs, the love that pumped through his veins, and the steadfastness that manifested in his presence.

And I've been lost without this. Utterly lost.

I've lost eight pounds from not having an appetite. I have a hard time falling asleep and getting out of bed and nothing is right anymore. I've wanted to go numb, give up, and today I drove an hour and a half away just to sit at a coffee shop where absolutely no one knew me. Because I don't have home anymore. I don't have the safety and stability that I never knew was such a big part of who I was.

I see patterns of this everywhere.

Like all the Disney movies in which leading characters lose their parents or are separated from them: *Tangled*, *Finding Nemo*, *Finding Dori*, *Frozen*, *Beauty and the Beast*, *Cinderella*, *Dumbo*, and the *Jungle Book*, to name a few. There's just something about when you lose home. It grabs at everyone's heart and makes for a heartwarming story when you make it wherever you find it.

"Who do you see in scripture who wished their story could have been written differently?" My mentor, Jessica, asked.

"Job," I responded. "David. Jesus. Paul."

Jessica added Joseph, Abraham, Stephen, and a few others.

What is this? If I'm real, I've only looked at the people around me whose lives seem good or full or untouched by the hurt that's touched mine and wondered why God loves them more than me. But what's also real is that salvation is not a ticket to a free and easy life. Real salvation is a hope that whispers, "I am with you," when everything around you is screaming the opposite. A real salvation is hiding behind the cross of a Savior who left His home too. He lived in the presence of God, in perfect peace, but somehow decided we were worth it. Let me assure, you I am not.

He was hunted and His life was at risk from the very first day. He was laid in an itchy, smelly, and uncomfortable stable, where He was probably ready to say, "God, I want to come home." But He didn't. He was so hard pressed on every side to carry with Him the weight of glory amidst such darkness and despair. He was alone, missing the home He had always known, just to be misunderstood, beaten, tortured, and mocked.

A real salvation is not being baptized into a life of safety. It is dying daily so that Christ can live, and that is difficult, exhausting, and at times you need to get away from it all, just like Jesus did.

Recently, I had a hard conversation with some of the ministry staff I work with. They shared they once worked on a staff where the pastor would say, "Okay, how many of you want to quit today?" And many would raise their hands. "Quit today," he would say, "but you can never give up."

I think a real salvation looks a lot more like this than the stories you see on Facebook about the person whose cancer shouldn't have been curable and yet they were saved, the family system that was so broken and was repaired. Yes, God is capable. But, He is the same God who worked through Joseph, Paul, and Silas throughout their imprisonment, through Naomi (Ruth's mother-in-law) losing her husband and son, through Stephen's stoning, and as much as I hate to claim it, through William Daryl Dalton's death on April 20, 2016.

The way of the cross is lonely. It's desolate and dark. It is often hopeless. I have needed friends to come alongside of me and carry the cross for me when I couldn't, and to believe the journey was worth it when I didn't. Some days it means your heart burning in your chest with pain and embracing much more profanity than you thought you ever would.

And it's only worth it because this isn't home. Because He will be my home. Because He is predictable, safe, and sure, even when I don't have the strength to believe it.

Real salvation doesn't mean being cynical. I'm trying not to tell myself I wouldn't be surprised if trial after trial is all that defines my life. Honestly, I am.

Real salvation means there is hope. There is a happy ending and a conclusion that overwhelmingly overshadows the present trials and afflictions that crush, overwhelm, and hurt. The way of the cross is real, and if it wasn't, there wouldn't be life. It's taken me a really long time to say that. I've wanted to see and feel God. To know that He is with me, somehow in it, and seeking to meet me in it. I've prayed unanswered prayers that walked me right to the edge of giving up.

I think that's what the way of the cross does, if Peter might say as he denied Jesus three times. But what has been real for me has been coming home to a Savior with merciful and gracious eyes, sitting at a well with room next to Him on the bench he's sitting on. A Savior who really sees my weakness. Who keeps breaking me from believing that what I have seen and known is all that there ever will be. Who holds me and calls me His beloved child and above all whispers, "I've missed home too."

A Real Father

We had spent a week in the hospital. I had received the call the Wednesday before my dad had a heart attack and spent many days waiting, praying, and hoping for his life. Then, we learned his brain damage was worse than expected. After he was taken off life support, we were moved to a new floor called "Palliative Care."

It was April 19, the day before my twenty-second birthday. All week I had prayed to hear my daddy's voice on my birthday. Everyone was praying he would go on the nineteenth so it wouldn't happen on my birthday. I was sitting on a terrible couch with my best friend Haven, who brought me a birthday gift. I had said I didn't want to see my dad lifeless. I wanted to remember him full of life and warm, so I told him goodbye before the ventilator was removed.

I went into the kitchen area to get some water and the nurse came with me, along with my mom. She introduced herself and shared the next day was her birthday as well. She told me she had lost her mom and now works on this floor where people come when they are at the end of their journey, especially those with cancer.

"People typically wait for either a specific person or event before they pass and I want to respect your decision, but you are both of those things to him right now." My body shook. I still can't put words to what I felt in that moment.

I knew I had to go back, so I told my discipleship leaders, Tracy and Tonja, who had been sitting with me. I went to the room where my dad's body was fighting for every last breath and asked my family to leave. It was just me and him. Well, his body really. I knew he wasn't there.

I've always loved princesses. My dad called me his "little princess girl" for longer than I can remember. I had a princess lunch box, princess ornaments, princess all things. And when William and Kate's royal wedding came around when I was in high school, I was bubbling over with enthusiasm. (Ask me what I did the day of the royal wedding for a laugh some day). I watched the wedding over and over, memorizing Kate's dress, the chapel, the flowers, everything so exquisite.

I looked for small details that I would want to be in my own wedding one day.

There was one moment I loved most. When Kate's dad walked her down the aisle, upon reaching the alter and handing her off, he took her hand, placed it on the clergy's hand, and then he joined their hands together. I thought the symbolism was so beautiful that a father hands his daughter to the Lord and He joins her with her husband. Beautiful.

At my dad's bedside on my birthday eve, I replayed that moment between Kate and her father in my head. I realized it was time for my dad to hand me off. But he needed me to let him. I stood at the foot of his bed, remembering all the thoughts I'd had that week. I remember the first time I saw him after his heart attack, when he squeezed my hands and his eyes fluttered when he heard my voice. I was so hopeful in that moment, but no longer.

I told him he had fought for me, loved me, and cared for me so well from my very first breath, and even before. That he had been the absolute best he could have been for me for twenty-two years. He had loved me sacrificially, unconditionally, and abidingly in the most beautiful way. He had cared for me well, and he could let me go. I knew he was fighting, and I told him to hand me over to Jesus, that I would be well taken care of and that he would always be my daddy.

The next day he took his last breath twenty-two years after the exact time I was born. He completed those twenty-two years. And it was the most beautiful way of hearing his voice when audibly I couldn't.

Those words weren't easy to say at the end of my dad's bed. They weren't easy to say, and they haven't been easy to feel. Not having my dad is really hard. It's hard and empty and hopeless.

And I have wanted God to be my Father, to step right in where my dad left off, which is hard to do. There have been moments when I have looked around and wondered, "Okay, who is going to do this now?" There have been broken lights and drawers that I haven't known how to fix, tires without air in them, and voids and emptiness in the everyday.

God being my Father has not meant Him filling every single gap my dad once did, but it has meant Him welcoming me home with Him, calling me His own, and reminding me that He will always take care of me.

This would have never been the journey I would have chosen to know God better, to know myself better, to know my friends better, or to be more real. But this is the one He has used. And as much as I would rewrite this ending all day long if I could, and as many days as the following sentence has been the very last thing I would ever believe, He is faithful. And that's real.

About the Author

My story began in a small town in southern Virginia. Every store we visited and restaurant we frequented were filled with familiar faces who all knew my name and my entire family. Cousins felt like siblings and aunts and uncles like second parents.

At eleven years old, my family moved to Spartanburg, South Carolina. Here I fell in love with volleyball, monograms, and student ministry. I began to feel a call to full time ministry and committed to walk in this direction that seems to consistently reshape at 16 years old.

Following high school, I attended Berry College in Rome, GA where I still call home. I received a Bachelor of

Arts in Psychology, minoring in Spanish and Women and Gender Studies. I now serve in my church, work in full time ministry with the WinShape College Program, and am pursuing a Master of Divinity.

Beyond my resumé, I think I have best grown to define myself as a mixture of Lorelai Gilmore (Gilmore Girls), Leigh Anne Tuohy (The Blind Side), and Mary Poppins. I love a strong cup of black coffee, all things chocolate peanut butter, and dancing at weddings.

CPSIA information can be obtained
at www.ICGtesting.com
Printed in the USA
BVHW081050050220
571501BV00004B/331

9 781642 795202